ADVANCE PRAISE FOR
Courage to Grow

"Acton Academy is on the vanguard of change in education in our country. After reading Laura's story, your first two questions will probably be, 'Why couldn't my school be like this?' and 'How can I send my kids to Acton?' This is an important story about learning what matters."

—SETH GODIN, AUTHOR OF *STOP STEALING DREAMS*

"Acton Academy is on the leading edge of what it means to give students agency of their own learning. What Laura has created is truly remarkable."

—SAL KHAN, FOUNDER OF KHAN ACADEMY

"Choosing an educational path for your children is the most important investment you will make as a parent. Laura's vision, courage, and profound insights on learning changed our lives and inspire us daily—her story will inspire you as well."

—DANI AND RUSS FOLTZ-SMITH, FOUNDERS AND PARENTS,
ACTON ACADEMY VENICE BEACH

"Acton Academy is one of the most important education developments in the world. The story behind the ideas, the school, and the movement is a must-read."

—TOM VANDER ARK, CEO OF GETTING SMART, PREVIOUSLY EXECUTIVE DIRECTOR
OF EDUCATION FOR THE BILL & MELINDA GATES FOUNDATION

"A remarkable book that captures the powerful journeys of Acton Academy's founders, students, parent community, and—I hope—the future of education around the globe. Any school, whether traditional or innovative, will gain insights from this magical place."

—TED DINTERSMITH, EDUCATION AUTHOR, FILM PRODUCER,
AND PHILANTHROPIST

"Acton Academy has transformed our family, inspiring each of us to find a calling and discover a Hero's Journey. Laura's book is a must-read for parents who long for a child to live up to his or her full potential."

—KIMBERLY WATSON-HEMPHILL, ACTON ACADEMY PARENT, AUTHOR OF *FAST
INNOVATION* AND FOUNDER AND CEO, FIREFLY CONSULTING

COURAGE

to

GROW

How Acton Academy
Turns Learning Upside Down

LAURA A. SANDEFER

This publication is designed to provide accurate and authoritative information in regard to the subject matter covered. It is sold with the understanding that the publisher and author are not engaged in rendering legal, accounting, or other professional services. If legal advice or other expert assistance is required, the services of a competent professional should be sought.

Cover design by Sheila Parr
Cover image © Shutterstock / Africa Studio

Cataloging-in-Publication data is available.

Print ISBN: 978-0-9995205-0-5

eBook ISBN: 978-0-9995205-1-2

Printed in the United States of America on acid-free paper

17 18 19 20 21 22   10 9 8 7 6 5 4 3 2 1

First Edition

To the founding Eagles, who had the courage to grow

Saskia

Sam

Chris

Bodhi

Cash

Charlie

Ellie

and to Taite, who was with us in spirit every step of the way

Follow the child.

—DR. MARIA MONTESSORI

CONTENTS

FOREWORD

If for nothing else, Acton Academy deserves respect for its singular role in steepening a famous S curve.

In their book *Disrupting Class*, Professor Clayton Christensen of Harvard Business School and his colleagues Michael Horn and Curtis Johnson claimed that online learning is a disruptive innovation that will transform the way the world learns. To illustrate this prediction, they drew an S-curve diagram, like the one that follows. Disruptive innovations follow an S-curve pattern, they said. The new technology creeps into the market slowly at first, as messy prototypes emerge. But then the substitution of the new technology for the old rises dramatically, until, finally, it approaches 100 percent of the market.

S curves are sometimes gradual, sometimes steep. When *Disrupting Class* was published in 2008, its authors were uncertain as to the slope of the curve that they expected. But one thing they knew: Online learning was following the pattern of a disruptive innovation. One day it would replace traditional classroom instruction.

That prediction was radical. Up until then, online learning was mostly a fringe alternative in K–12 education, embraced by homeschooling families who were okay with being "distance learners," remote from campus.

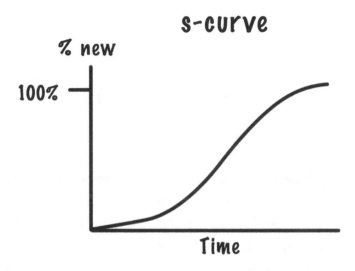

By the time I joined the Clayton Christensen Institute a few years later, however, the S curve was beginning to veer up, thanks to the arrival of blended learning—the combination of online learning and brick-and-mortar schooling. By 2011, we counted forty school districts, charter school networks, independent schools, and virtual schools in the United States that were delivering blended learning rather than traditional instruction. One of the forty was an unusual micro-school in Austin, Texas, called Acton Academy.

At first my interest in Acton Academy was entirely academic. Along with the thirty-nine other pioneering organizations, Acton Academy was steepening the slope on the S curve right before our eyes. Distance learning had reached a plateau. For online learning to get any bigger, it would need to take on some of the jobs that brick-and-mortar schools do—jobs like providing custodial care, face-to-face mentoring, social experiences, and sports. By combining the disruptive innovation of online learning with select elements of the incumbent system, these forty organizations were following the disruptive innovation playbook to the letter. A few, including Acton Academy, had business models that were primed to scale well. That was important. It meant that the trajectory for the disruption was on path. What was once a radical prediction now had forty live examples to manifest that the heralded transformation of brick-and-mortar schools had begun—and was poised for growth.

What's more, Acton Academy stood out from the others. It had a "Flex" blended-learning model, in which online learning is the backbone of much of the core instruction and the primary role of the face-to-face teacher is to guide, encourage, and activate learning, not to deliver instruction. Several other schools among the forty had Flex models, but Acton Academy was the only one that figured out how to do a Flex model with elementary-aged children. Finding Acton Academy was like spotting Bigfoot.

LEADING THE DISRUPTION

Fast-forward several years and Acton Academy continues to be a decade ahead of the rest. Although thousands of schools today have disruptive, blended models, Jeff and Laura Sandefer's school—which has become a global network—stands apart for its unusually successful and counterintuitive approach to doing school.

According to Christensen, one benefit of disruptive innovations is that they distribute access to people at the margins. Imagine a series of concentric circles, like in the diagram that follows.

Each circle represents a population of people who can access a product or service. Only people with the most wealth and expertise have access at the center. The larger circles represent people with less wealth and expertise; most everyday folks live out here. Disruptive innovations push access to this outer rim. Think TurboTax and Amazon Prime, for example—two disruptions that push access out to the average Joes.

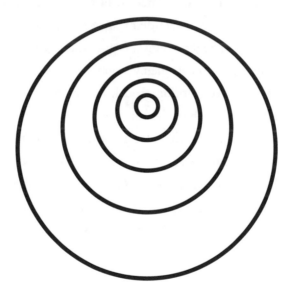

From their tiny original schoolhouse, the Sandefers intuited that the disruptive innovation of online learning has similar power to push out access to the people with the very least wealth and expertise of all—children. That insight allowed them to pioneer several breakthrough school design choices. Most importantly, Acton Academy empowers children with the habits, mentors, online lessons, and tracking system that they need to be able to manage their own learning. That delegation of control helps the children develop agency—the ability to make choices. Observe Acton Academy for a scant minute and the first thing you'll notice is the stunning sense of student buy-in and self-efficacy. It's because of all that agency.

Giving students ownership, in turn, frees up adults to serve as guides and mentors. It flips the mentor-to-student ratio from 1-to-many to 1-to-1. Children don't get lost at Acton Academy. Human connection overflows from the system as the entire community works together to decide on the rules, sign off on each other's badges, peer-critique projects, and build cool things.

FROM ACADEMIC TO PERSONAL

A few months after finishing that early blended-learning report, I scheduled a visit to Acton Academy and brought along my husband, Allan. That's when things became personal.

It's one thing to understand Acton Academy in theory. It's another thing entirely to step inside its walls and feel with one's heart what sound design, true principles, and lovely execution do for the well-being and joyfulness of children. That's when my own family's lives changed forever.

You're in for a treat as you read Laura Sandefer's story of how Acton Academy came to be. Her campuses share the grace, wisdom, and whole-heartedness that Laura embodies herself. Be forewarned, however, that if you're anything like hundreds of parents and me, once you discover how much children can do in an environment that dignifies, magnifies, and inspires their minds to learn, there's no going back to traditional classrooms again.

—Heather Staker

INTRODUCTION

"I can't draw," I said to my husband, Jeff.

"Yes, you can," he said. "Turn the image you are trying to draw upside down. Now draw exactly what you see. Your left brain quiets down. Its rational language and organizing directives will allow your right brain to take over, releasing you from your judging, analytical self. No longer will you feel bound by 'it's a chair' and feel the stress to draw the perfect chair. Try it!"

This exercise, developed in the late 1970s by Betty Edwards and written up in her book *Drawing on the Right Side of the Brain*, changed everything about my understanding of learning to draw. I discovered a new part of myself by turning the image of my subject matter upside down.

This change of perspective reminded me of Maria Montessori's insistence on having "fresh eyes" each day when working with children—the ability to strip one's own judgment and to observe clearly and freshly, so the person being observed remains free from your prejudices, opinions, and moods.

It is with this spirit of embracing new perspectives that Jeff and I entered the world of education in 2008: upside down and with fresh eyes.

We are products of America's public school system. We each

have memories of that "magical teacher" who changed our lives. We each received graduate degrees from traditional, private universities. And we each pursued education as a part of our own professional paths.

Despite our backgrounds in education, we never set out to start our own school or design something brand new in the K–12 realm. It was only when we had children of our own that things changed. We understood the world our children would face would be vastly different—unimaginably so—from the world we encountered as young adults. We knew they'd need to be armed to know how to learn, respond, innovate, and create in their own way rather than become skilled at taking tests and following instructions like we had. We believed our children would need the light of curiosity burning brightly in their eyes—not just when they were young learners, but throughout their childhood, teen years, and far beyond.

A small, quiet voice started creeping into our hearts as we looked for school options that would equip them for this wide-open, futuristic territory for which we had no compass. What had worked for us as children looked desperately outdated, impractical, and simply wrong, even with good, smart people working hard to make the traditional schools adaptive to today's opportunities.

With no map or long-term strategic plan, we set out in the way artists and scientists do—disciplining ourselves to let go of preconceived ideas, experimenting without demanding outcomes, and using clear principles with standards of excellence to constrain us at every turn. Our goal? To create and bring to life a vision of "school" that worked for our own children and anyone who would join us. We didn't want to disrupt or compete with traditional public or private schools. We wanted to run parallel to them.

While we sought data and results, our journey was fueled by a power not mentioned in academic spheres as part of the education equation.

Like all parents, we were driven by love. Love of the human spirit, of freedom, of learning, of risky adventure, and of responsibility. Love for our own children and the light in their eyes.

We wondered: Can a vision of school rationally encounter the power of love and claim it?

We found: only when the vision of school is turned upside down.

Acton Academy is the outcome of our dreaming and scheming. It is a new vision of what a learning community can be. It is gritty and dreamy. It is not for the faint of heart, because it inspires growth and transformation—neither of which are achieved without some suffering, which is the Latin root of the word *passion.*

With almost a decade under our belts, we can claim that Acton's method of learning works. We have proof, which I will reveal in the pages ahead.

This book is the story of Acton Academy's origin. Although it began as an ambitious extension of homeschooling, Acton has now grown into a worldwide community of over 800 students in more than sixty locations in eight countries, and it's growing every week. Many communities are small—not more than 7 to 10 students—because they have only recently opened. The more mature locations are nearing a maximum size of 120 young people and are already spawning new communities. We currently have 5,300 applications in our pipeline from parents around the world wanting to open one for their own children. Our small school is set up as a not-for-profit 501(c)(3) organization driven by efficiency and accountability in operations so that the focus remains on our mission.

Our school model includes Socratic questions to hone deep thinking; peer teaching; apprenticeships for real-world learning; and state-of-the-art online learning for mastering the basics of reading, grammar, and math. Hands-on projects designed with game-theory incentives deliver opportunities for young people to dig into the arts, sciences, world history, and economics. Although we can translate the achievements of our students into a traditional transcript that proves mastery, the end goal of learning at Acton isn't to get a good score on a test or an A from a teacher. It is something quite different and includes solving real problems, analyzing moral dilemmas, making difficult decisions, persuading audiences to action, creating innovative opportunities for the world, resolving personal conflicts, and even making and managing money.

The ultimate goal, though, is to *learn how to learn*, *learn how to do*, and *learn how to be*, so that each person who enters our doors will find a calling and change the world. Each person who graduates from an Acton Academy will be equipped to master the next step in their life plan with gusto—whether it be attending a fine university, taking a gap year to travel, or starting a business.

As I take you through our story, you'll experience the physical environment of Acton, which is designed like a one-room schoolhouse, with ages mixed so that peers can learn from and teach one other. You'll also experience the emotional engagement of our young people and taste how freedom feels for children. Because there are mountains of stories and experiences I could share from these years, I've had to condense the pieces, moving some of the projects and discussions out of chronological order. But the tale is true and yours for the taking.

Some people say what we are doing isn't really all that different. True, there are excellent school models in the public and private sectors emerging around the country that use similar approaches, including teachers who are fueled by love for children and learning.

But there are a few distinguishing aspects of Acton that separate us from any other school model, and they are the reason for our strong outcomes. They also cause consternation in those who witness Acton in action. It's hard to believe it's real until you see it.

Our biggest point of separation is the upside-down power structure that pushes control and decision making to the children. We have few adults serving as bureaucratic authority figures around our learning environments. We believe adults in such capacity can stymie learning and that peers have more power. Because of this, we are free from the traditional trappings that have come to be known as "school." Acton Academy has no teachers, only guides. No report cards, only student-earned badges and portfolios to prove mastery of skills. No classrooms, only creative work spaces called studios. No assigned homework, only what a child chooses to continue doing at home. No attendance requirements. No bureaucracy, only a lean machine that drives the cost of private schooling down to lower costs than any model we've seen.

Read on; you'll be surprised.

Visit an Acton Academy and you won't hear an announcement over an intercom by a principal, nor will you see a teacher managing behavior at recess. You won't hear buzzers marking the end of math work time or science class.

This radical power shift does not mean children are running wild with no accountability or discipline, although there are days when chaos reigns. The Acton story is most surprising in that this power shift unleashes children to care so deeply about their learning that they choose to work hard, hold tight boundaries for each other, and rise to excellence in ways we never imagined. Self-imposed rigor is integral to our daily life.

Acton Academy is grounded in trusting children and believing they can handle big responsibilities. "It's always opposite day at Acton," an eight-year-old named Ian told me one day.

Through the ambiguity and messiness of life and learning, which we adults tend to abhor, we see children rise up and embrace the mindset of heroes—people who take responsibility for their choices, get back up after falling down, and refuse to quit even when it's hard. We see children learning how to learn and loving it.

A second distinguishing characteristic of our school brings vibrancy to the upside-down canvas we've painted. It's the landscape on which our curriculum is grounded and is our "why" behind everything that happens in a day, week, or year. It is the Hero's Journey.

This grand mythological narrative of an ordinary person leaving a place of comfort to meet a challenge describes what all humans since the beginning of time have yearned for in life. We crave a life that means something to the world. We crave being known for our uniqueness, not what others expect or hope us to be. The Hero's Journey beckons each of us to answer the questions: Who am I? Why am I here? Will I step forward to answer the call to adventure—knowing there will be monsters to battle, dark valleys to cross, and mountains to climb? Will I be passive or active about the direction of my life? Can I find the treasure of my potential, the holy grail, and return home with it to help others? Disney uses this narrative well to draw young hearts in, as do all great writers and storytellers. The Hero's Journey crosses cultures and binds us as a tribe.

Children at Acton Academy know *why* they are being challenged to learn, to master, to solve, to forgive, to apologize, to discuss. They are doing so because it is part of their personal quest—their Hero's Journey—to find their greatest treasures, their inner gifts, and hone them in order to solve a burning need in their community, city, or world.

At Acton, we talk about this magnificent journey often. Whether it's learning multiplication or engaging in a heated match of GaGa ball, there is a clear and important reason that urges us forward. People in our community—from six-year-olds to sixty-year-olds—embrace the challenge to learn and grow, knowing there will be suffering along the way because it's part of the journey. For this reason, we arm ourselves with courage each day. The courage to grow.

This is just the beginning of our story in many ways. Part of the magic of the Acton journey is its ever-changing, ever-evolving nature—and the awakening it inspires not just in children of all creeds and backgrounds but also in their parents.

The pages that follow will take you along on our quest to create a unique learning community. You'll get a firsthand tour, and then we'll drop back in time to reveal how our story truly unfolded—in an unglamorous, plodding fashion with stumbles, failures, joys, tears, and victories. As we strove to create a school that was free to look at learning from a different viewpoint, we met friends, heroes, guides, and foes—all in very unlikely places. It may feel messy at times because it was and still is.

This is not a how-to book. Nor is it a book about educational theory. It's simply our tale of surprise and discovery, of our growing pains through trial and error to the point where our fundamental beliefs about education were transformed and our creation, Acton Academy, was poised for expansive growth. And like all good tales, there is a surprise ending—a bit of magic about parenting and living that has changed our family and countless others forever.

I've learned much along the way. One of my favorite lessons grew from answering a question posed to me by Socratic master teacher Steven Tomlinson, who asked, "Would you rather be right or surprised?"

I began this journey wanting to be right. I wanted formulas, answers, evidence. I even wanted report cards, test scores, and grades—some authority figure to tell me how I was doing.

I now am grateful to be surprised. With surprise comes a sense of wonder, a sense of risk and flying off into the unknown, ready to self-correct when needed. Embracing school as an experiment has meant we are all learners at Acton; there are no experts among us. There is a playful and fun yet deeply serious ethos that surrounds us each day, because we are bound by principles and purpose. We can be free to explore with a sense of stability in our questioning and questing.

Can you free yourself enough from your own past school experiences to see things upside down? Are you one of the people who will claim a grand adventure for your family or, if necessary, start your own Acton Academy? At the very least, this story may inspire you to be still and listen to that small, quiet voice in your heart. It's quite possible the fate of a free society—and your children's future—depends on your answer to the question: Will you join us?

Let me draw a new picture for you.

Chapter 1

A DAY *in the* LIFE *of* ACTON ACADEMY

"The Acton community and life experience provide our son the best possible environment in which to develop. You empower kids to an unparalleled degree. We truly believe this, relative to all other educational options. Every Acton parent goes to sleep each night thankful for the opportunity to be in this moment."

—CHARLIE AND PAM MADERE, ACTON ACADEMY PARENTS

It was the spring of 2011. Acton Academy's second year was in full swing. The Staker family had never stepped foot in Texas. "We just had to see Acton Academy for ourselves," Allan Staker said as he described his memory of that day when he and his wife, Heather, flew to Austin for one day and one reason.

They wanted to see if what they had heard about our school was true. Heather, a leading expert in innovative schools, had been visiting hundreds of classrooms across the nation, meeting with teachers, administrators, and thought leaders to collect evidence of best practices.

"We pulled down the narrow downtown street and paid for parking. It was very close to downtown, but still felt like a quiet little side street. There was not a lot of traffic. The house was so cute! Tiny, in fact, with a beautiful Acton Academy sign out front. Beautiful trees lined the street and there was lots of shade on the property. A bridge from the street's sidewalk led to the front door. Heather had toured many schools before, but this was a first for me. But I've been a student and a parent, and I knew what schools were supposed to look like and how kids were supposed to act. I had no idea what I was in for.

"Laura, you met us at the door and guided us into the main room to the round green rug, where the students were having a morning discussion. We quietly sat in chairs at the back. The students sat in a neat circle, all looking at each other. No one was goofing off or causing trouble—they were all engaged.

"It's easy to forget this now, but the students were all very young—there was no middle school or high school yet. They fit the size of the tiny, adorable building. I think there were fifteen to twenty of them.

"The kids were having a Socratic discussion about which games should or shouldn't be played at recess. Raised hands, well-organized thoughts, and a surprising, quiet intensity—all about something as trivial as Four-Square," continued Allan. He went on to describe what they saw, which remains etched in his memory.

"This went on for several minutes. It was fascinating—I didn't know kids in groups were capable of that. I noticed right away that there was very little input from the guides—only suggestions and concessions among the students, and then the business was concluded.

"After the discussion, the guides dismissed the students for project time. I'm not sure what I expected here, but what happened next was fascinating. The students quietly stood up, and then two by two, and without the slightest bit of grown-up guidance (or coercion!), the pairs each moved to a different station. It couldn't have been choreographed better: One pair sat down at tiny desks to go to work on their potato clock. Another pair moved to the Lego Mindstorms set and resumed work on the robot they were programming. Another pair sat next to each other, opened their laptops, and began scanning YouTube videos about something related to a project they were working on. Another set logged in to Khan Academy and got started on math. Each pair was doing a completely different activity! And they did it in a quiet, happy, self-guided way.

"And the guides? They acted like all of this was completely normal. They just stood and watched the show. I remember the students had *lab coats*. They were all hanging on hooks in the kitchen. I think that was one of the details that sealed it for us. These children were engaged in a simulation of Thomas Edison's lab!

"Every room of that little house was full of light and beautifully stocked with educational goodness—but neatly so, as if the set dressers from *Mister Rogers' Neighborhood* were doing a spread for *Real Simple* magazine. Globes and toys and a goldfish and books . . . everything but the trolley.

"Every room felt like someplace where you'd want to just sit and learn. It was the perfect place for a kid to spend each day. There was a mural painted by the children on the fence lining the property. It was colorful, playful, and happy.

"As we pictured our own kids here, Heather and I were just beaming. We knew there was an application deadline the following day. As we sat at the airport awaiting our flight home, we quickly downloaded the books we needed to have read as part of your entry process. We spent the entire flight home filling out our applications. We pulled our kids out of school the next day to complete theirs. When we were accepted, I scrambled to find a job that would move us to Austin."

Heather added to the memory. "I remember Allan's total head-over-heels attraction to everything we saw. I also remember sitting in the Austin airport looking at each other and knowing at the same time what we needed to do, like it was destiny.

"From my perspective, there were two novelties that hit me as we first observed Acton Academy that day. The first was that you discovered, before any other schools I'd seen, that the disruptive innovation of online learning pushes control to students in a way that fundamentally rethinks children's capacity. If children have the capacity to learn via online delivery of instruction, then why not get adults out of the way and equip the children to go for it! I was amazed to see how liberally you embraced that idea, and yet it worked. Guides were on hand to activate the learning, but the children had adapted to do the rest of it without adult helicoptering. The liberation and empowerment for children were breathtaking.

"Second, I was amazed by your environment. Each corner of that house—from the kitchen tools to the reading nooks to the robotics corner to the homemade hula-hoops in the backyard— was designed to prime curiosity, experimentation, and the joy of childhood. It looked like the better Finnish schools that get so much acclaim today. We couldn't keep our own children in a conventional school any longer—no more conventional lessons, no more conventional playground equipment, no more teaching children to put a bubble in their mouths to stay quiet while they stand in line. Innovations that distribute power to the power-less have changed the equation, and you discovered this at Acton Academy, at least a decade ahead of the pack."

. . .

Heather Staker was a young luminary in the world of innovative education. As a high school senior in Irvine, California, she had served on the state board of education. She attended Harvard Business School and studied under Clayton Christensen, ulti-mately partnering with him in late 2010 to cowrite a report on the newest innovation in education—online learning—and how schools were capturing technology to serve students. As part of her research in writing this report, she and a fellow cowriter, Matt Clayton, called Jeff to interview him about Acton Academy. Little did we know this phone call would lead to the Stakers' trip to Texas a few months later.

Jeff had followed Christensen's work on disruptive innovation with great interest and agreed to a fifteen-minute phone conversa-tion. When they got off the phone, they had spoken for more than the fifteen minutes he'd agreed to. It was more like ninety minutes.

Staker asked a few questions, but mostly she listened as Jeff described Acton's goal of pushing control to the students, allow-ing them to progress at their own pace and interact as a com-munity of learners. He described the school's underpinnings and its adherence to Socratic teaching—as well as its use of several online learning programs, including DreamBox, Rosetta Stone, and Learning Today.

When Jeff thought they were finished, there was a moment of silence on the other end.

"Can I ask you a personal question, not connected to the study?" Staker asked.

"Sure," Jeff replied.

"Would you consider letting my husband and me be the first people to start an Acton Academy in California? This is by far the most exciting school I've studied, and I want something like this for our children."

Heather and Allan had four children at the time and were living in Honolulu, Hawaii, but were considering a move to the mainland, with their eyes on California. Their eldest child was just starting elementary school.

Jeff called me after hanging up with Heather and said, "Congratulations. Your school is captivating the best minds in education. Be ready to create a prototype kit so others can follow your lead. We'll be receiving a copy of Heather Staker's report soon. It'll be interesting to see how she describes Acton Academy in comparison to other schools."

Follow my lead? I was building the airplane as we were flying it, as Jeff liked to say.

Acton Academy was only two years old and it was already nearing full capacity at thirty-six elementary students (see appendix A). Word had spread that our students had progressed three grade levels, on average, on the national standardized test we delivered—and this was after only nine months in our program. The more seductive secret, though, was that the children at Acton loved learning. Our secret was out.

But I wasn't thinking about what the rest of the world

wanted. I was simply focused on creating an engaging and challenging learning journey for the young children at Acton Academy. There was something happening within the walls of our tiny, adorable house. It was joyful learning. Could we bottle this up? In a kit? For others to use?

I didn't have time to think about that. The morning's Socratic discussion was about to begin.

. . .

Libby finished reading aloud the newspaper article and looked at the group of fellow students sitting on the floor in the circle around her. She'd just explained the premise for today's Socratic discussion, which she had blended from different sources to give a complete picture of the issue:

There were whales trapped in Arctic ice. They had only small holes to breathe through, and the holes were shrinking as the ice refroze. The open ocean was too far for them to reach in a single breath. The whales would drown as soon as the shelf above them solidified.

Three commercial ships were also stuck in ice, their crews near starvation and hypothermia. They weren't able to free themselves and couldn't travel over the ice to safety.

There were icebreakers near enough to help, but time was limited for both the whales and the ship crews.

"If you're the dispatcher for the icebreakers," Libby asked, "what do you do? Do you send them to save the ships or the whales?"

The young students called on each other, agreeing and

disagreeing, specifying the reason for their opinion and building on each other's statements. A consensus was building around the possibility of saving them both if they worked fast enough.

Libby was ready to turn up the heat. "There is one more important piece of information. The weather is worsening quickly. It's impossible to save both the whales and the humans with these conditions. Which do you choose to save: the whales or the humans?"

The debate about the ethics of saving one over the other became more emotional but remained respectful and clear.

"There are plenty of humans in the world," Ellie said. "Isn't it more important to save the whales?"

"But can we just let people die?" Chris asked.

"These whales are included on the endangered species list," Anaya said, pointing to the whiteboard.

There were thirty-six students in the group. Libby stopped the discussion and took a vote. It was a tie: Half of them wanted to save the whales, and the other half wanted to save the humans. The debate continued.

In perfect Socratic form, Libby didn't relent. She held up her finger to signal there was more information coming.

She said, "There are 20 whales still alive in the ice and 1,000 people on the boat."

This seemed to sway the group toward resolution, and the energy of the discussion abated.

Libby continued to turn up the heat to reignite the intensity of the conflict.

"These are the only 20 gray whales left in the world," she said.

The students leaned in. This changed everything. Then she delivered the final punch: "And your family is on the boat."

Libby's questions—creating a fictional moral dilemma based on a real situation—did exactly what the Socratic method aims to do: force hard choices, change minds based on analysis of information, and instill the skill of careful listening and concise, purposeful communicating.

After five more minutes of heated but clear arguments, Libby looked at the clock. In pure commitment to the Socratic rules, she knew it was time to close the discussion.

"One final vote. Please raise your hand if you'd save the humans." She counted. "Who would save the whales?"

It was clear. The humans had won this one.

"Thank you all for your participation. We have time for two people to share why they changed their minds and any lessons learned from the discussion." With a small smile of satisfaction, she closed the group right on time. The students stood up, giving her a round of applause. She had led them through rough intellectual and emotional territory with an air of professional elegance. They, too, were satisfied. All dispersed to their desks to begin their independent work time.

Libby was nine years old at the time. There was not a teacher in the room as she facilitated the discussion, nor did an adult choose the topic, advise her, collect the research, or write the questions. The ages of the children in the circle ranged from six to ten years old.

. . .

On most days, Acton Academy functions like a well-ordered society, as well-run as any small town in America with a functioning government, laws, and a finely tuned economy, with each person contributing a special gift or skill.

On other days, the leaders don't rise up, and small distractions descend into chaos. These days include moments of gut-wrenching frustration as we adults have to force ourselves to step back more than once—and maybe more than twice—to let the children solve their own problems.

I didn't start with a natural inclination to step back when my children were having a problem to let them figure it out on their own. You practically had to chain me down to stop me from running out to tie their shoes so they wouldn't trip, or rush home to get their backpacks when they forgot them, or tell the mean kid on the playground to be nice to my child.

I did not fully understand the leap I would have to make in my own mind and heart to trust the children to handle struggles and even suffer in order to grow into highly functioning, intelligent, and kind humans. It would be a full decade before the urgency of this lesson would hit home.

And it all began with a seemingly innocuous conversation with a teacher in the hallway of one of the top traditional private schools in Austin, Texas.

CHAPTER 2

A CALL *to* ACTION

"Sheila and I are blessed that you and Jeff took the initiative to start this excellent learning environment. We could not imagine a better place to equip our children for the future."

—HERB AND SHEILA SINGH, ACTON ACADEMY PARENTS

Like every Tuesday afternoon back in 2007, Jeff, in his dark blue suit and red tie, picked up Taite, our oldest child (whom we shared with her mother), drove home, and walked across the gravel driveway to our house. Taite, ten years old, spunky, and engaging, skipped behind him, her school uniform disheveled from the day. As Jeff got closer, I could see something dark in his expression. He was usually excited to spend treasured time with Taite; something was wrong.

"We're not doing this anymore," he said quietly.

"Not doing *what*?" I asked, just as five-year-old Charlie and four-year-old Sam pushed past us out the kitchen door to get to Taite, their favorite person on earth. It was a gorgeous April afternoon and the green grass beckoned. The children ran off into the yard, our three dogs barking wildly behind them. Jeff and I slumped onto the porch steps together, and I waited for him to continue.

"We're not doing this school thing anymore," he said. He watched the kids play.

I wasn't sure where this was coming from. Taite was happy in her traditional elementary school, and the boys were in a fine Montessori school; they were still too young for elementary school, but we had started thinking about where we should enroll them.

Jeff explained.

When he picked up Taite, he dropped in to talk with her math teacher. He told him we were looking at more mainstream options for Sam and Charlie, who up to that point had, in their Montessori school, choices about what to work on during the day and lots of opportunity for movement.

Jeff asked, "How soon should we move them to a more traditional school?"

The teacher said, "As soon as possible."

Jeff asked why, and the teacher said, "Once they've had that much freedom, they'll hate being chained to a desk and being talked to all day."

Jeff couldn't help himself. "I wouldn't blame them!"

The teacher looked down at the floor, and Jeff was worried he'd offended him. When he looked up, there were tears in the teacher's eyes.

This teacher, known as the best teacher in the school, said, "I wouldn't either."

Jeff turned and looked at me. "Laura, I'm done," he said. "Charlie and Sam can learn without being trapped at a desk all day. We have to find another alternative. We've talked about how much the world has changed since we went to school. We need to either homeschool or create our own school."

We'd chosen a Montessori program for the boys because we'd studied Maria Montessori's work and believed in the science behind her design of giving children choices in their work, along with clear boundaries. But our school didn't have an upper-elementary program, so we knew we'd need to make a change one day soon. Sadly, our options all looked pretty much the same, just like what we ourselves had gone through in our schooling. But the world was so different now with smart phones, the Human Genome Project, and Google, for starters. What would learning in the twenty-first century look like if you started with a blank sheet of paper?

We were hearing a call to action—the starting point of every Hero's Journey since the beginning of time.

Looking back to look forward

Jeff and I weren't sure what the future of learning would look like, but we had a roadmap of what worked in the past. America hasn't always had a mega-education industry. In fact, it all started with integrated one-room schoolhouses and practical apprenticeships. By the late nineteenth century, the United States had become the strongest country on earth *without* a centralized education system. Reading, writing, and math were delivered in one-room schoolhouses, where children of all ages largely learned from each other. The great hero stories of the world— education through character-driven allegory—were pillars, as were the rags-to-riches Horatio Alger stories that made individual effort part of our American DNA. Only a few of the elite went to college, to study law or join the clergy. Young people learned to do something that mattered in a master–apprentice system. Learning to know—acquiring rote knowledge, which was repeated and memorized—was valued, especially because books were expensive and hard to come by. But learning to *do* and learning to *be* were also valued. Together, competence and character mattered more than simply knowledge. In the complex evolution and growth of public and private schools in our country, more and more standardization of content necessitated, relying on tests to prove learning and categorize children based on test scores. We wondered if it might be possible to retrieve what had been lost in the process.

The opportunity fascinated us. Having learned the Socratic method during his time at Harvard Business School, Jeff had been teaching with it at the graduate level. I had studied cognition and learning to receive my master's in education from Vanderbilt University's Peabody College. It had always been in my heart to become a public school teacher. We were enthralled with learning about the history of education and excited by the explosion of technology. With digital libraries and online courses readily available and inexpensive, we could bring every great lecturer, expert, and teacher right into the room. At the same time, using innovative education games—or "gamification"—was erupting around us and was clearly here to stay. This meant technology and education experts were integrating game mechanics with curriculum content to make learning more engaging and fun. In SimCity, for example, children learn the basics of civil engineering and how to think like a mayor to understand city planning. We saw endless opportunities to transform what "curriculum" looked like and make the learning experience as captivating as a game—one that feels almost addictive, focusing your attention so that time seems to disappear.

We took a deep breath and decided to cross the threshold into unknown territory.

Glimpsing a new vision of learning

We knew we were going to veer off the traditional track for our children's schooling but had no clear idea what this new path would look like. Jeff, who had been ranked by *BusinessWeek* and *The Economist* as one of the top entrepreneurship professors in the country while teaching at the University of Texas, founded the Acton School of Business, naming this specialized MBA program after the Victorian scholar and philosopher, Lord John D. Acton.

Lord Acton's writings about liberty and learning served the entrepreneurship mission well. Acton famously wrote, "Power tends to corrupt. Absolute power corrupts absolutely." Lord Acton's deepest work was focused on the relationship between liberty and morality. He envisioned a community that is free *and* virtuous. His principles included striving for excellence and giving unselfishly for the good of the community.

We, too, envisioned a community for the youngest learners—as young as five and six years old—that would be bound by principles of freedom, excellence, and moral goodness. The

Acton name helped us take our dreams from lofty ideals to concrete truths.

What's in a name?

Calling ourselves "Acton Academy" quickly forced the delineation of our own core values and principles of learning. We decided to cobble together what we knew would work with what we thought would work and experiment with it. If it didn't work, we'd try something different.

Some of our best ideas came from our children, gathered around the dinner table. One night as we dug into tacos and shared our personal highs and lows from the day, Sam lit up. "Let's do a fair! Like a science one but with businesses."

This sounded interesting. Since having the inkling to start our own school, we'd been giving Charlie, Taite, and Sam some big projects at home to help us understand how they learn, what hooked them, and what resources we could draw from. One of these home projects was entrepreneurship, Jeff's area of expertise. They'd been practicing with variations of lemonade stands on our street corner, learning the difference between profit and revenue and how to make operational decisions through an online game called "Robo Rush." This game was created for graduate-level students, yet our young children were playing it and learning from it. This surprised and enlightened us.

Our dinner conversation had moved from sharing how our days went to focusing on this question: "How can you prove you've learned something without taking a test?"

"You just do it," Taite said. Her words had sparked Sam's idea of a fair. With it fresh on the table, Jeff and I started rattling off names we thought would be catchy. How about the Young Entrepreneurs Expo? The Entrepreneurship Exhibition?

Charlie jumped in. "Just call it what it is. It's a Children's Business Fair."

So clear. So simple. He was exactly right. With that, we decided to host a Children's Business Fair in our yard. We'd create flyers, make a simple website, and invite other children to join in the fun.

After dinner, Jeff and I realized something obvious but often overlooked when it comes to education. We must involve the children in decision making about their learning experiences. They can be trusted to be creative and direct. Their participation inspires a feeling of ownership and pride. Plus, they have amazing ideas—much better than ours.

Thus began our claiming of core values for "Acton Academy."

FIRST, TRUST THE CHILDREN

It is a truth that the Founding Fathers knew—that children need guardrails, mentors, and legitimate authority, and they could be trusted with far more responsibility than most school administrators today could imagine. At least as we had experienced it.

Such trusting of children came easily to Jeff and me. I learned it from my parents, who moved my family from coast to coast and in between during my childhood. My father, a renowned pastor, and my mother, a beloved science teacher, knew the best learning came through being free to explore the world, holding real jobs at an early age, and asking deep questions of mentors. They trusted my three sisters and me from a very early age.

Jeff learned the same lessons by listening to Sugata Mitra share his stories and research about children teaching themselves when left alone, without adult intervention.

This simple idea of trusting the children with freedom and responsibility would become the secret ingredient for Acton Academy.

THEN, LET THEM STRUGGLE

It's much easier to think objectively about letting children struggle to solve their own problems than to carry out those thoughts with my own hands and feet as a mother. When I see my children hurting, my maternal instincts can get warped, and I swoop in to fix things for them—even when I know they can do it themselves.

On an intellectual level, Jeff and I knew struggling was valuable in terms of real learning and growth. Our new school culture needed to embrace the importance of learning from failure—not avoiding it. Ours would not be a "trophy for everyone" environment. But could we find parents who would let their children struggle, fail, even suffer in order to grow? Could *I* be that kind of parent?

Madeline Levine wrote in *The Price of Privilege*, "Parents who persistently fall on the side of intervening for their child, as opposed to supporting their child's attempts to problem-solve, interfere with the most important task of childhood and adolescence: the development of a sense of self."

How could I possibly ask other parents to step back if I couldn't do it myself? This truth would need to become part of my daily life as a mom so I could better support others who would join Acton Academy.

AND ALWAYS, SEIZE THE ADVENTURE

Questions, curiosity, trust, struggle—these are the ultimate traits of a real adventure. As the pieces to our puzzle lined up, we realized Acton Academy was more a quest to discover one's greatest gifts and the grand wonders of the world than a "school." This led us to pursue a deeper understanding of the Hero's Journey.

Since the dawn of human civilization, the great myth affirming life as an adventure of self-discovery has struck souls of all ages. Joseph Campbell's work brought the truth behind this narrative to life. George Lucas and Disney have used it well. From *Star Wars* to *The Lion King* and *Beauty and the Beast*, their stories hinge on the truth that even young children are drawn to transformative questions:

· Am I really a match for this task?

· Can I overcome the dangers?

· Who are my friends?

· Do I have the courage and the capacity for the challenge before me?

Each of us is just an ordinary person; but if we're willing to say yes to new experiences and keep moving forward, even when it's hard, it hurts, and it includes failure, then we are—all of us— heroes on a journey.

Our decision was made. Acton Academy would be an invitation to a real-life Hero's Journey. The courage to say yes to the journey would be the starting point for each child and parent.

Gathering a solid foundation of mentors

During the months that followed, Jeff and I sought out heroes in education. We hoped our research into these heroes would help us gain deeper insights into what did and didn't work in children's education.

One of those was Oliver DeMille, author of *A Thomas Jefferson Education: Teaching a Generation of Leaders for the Twenty-First Century*. We invited him to Austin and soon found ourselves sitting with him over iced tea in our living room.

"My family had great expectations for me," he said, his long arms draped across the back of our couch. "I was sociable and inquisitive, and they lovingly believed I would excel at everything I tried. But I could not learn to read."

His family had no television, and his parents read to each of their kids for hours. His parents were even teachers in his school. Still, he couldn't read.

"The school district performed extensive testing and decided that I needed to be included in the special-education class for students with special learning needs. I was confused and worried as I left my classmates and joined this 'special' class."

It wasn't long until his father came to the door of the class and motioned for him to join him in the hall. "My dad took me by the hand, led me to the advanced class, opened the door, and simply said: 'You belong in here.' With those four words he changed my life."

His parents continued to work with him at home, and through several years of difficulty and patience, Oliver became a fluent reader. This experience helped him develop one of his core beliefs.

"My father was the one who believed that no one should be a teacher unless he or she believes that each child is a genius," he told us. "His belief in me is why I am who I am."

And then he repeated his gold nugget of advice: "No one should be a teacher unless he believes every child is a genius."

Every child is a genius. Radical, wonderful, and quite upside-down from the current labeling and classification of children at every turn. It felt natural to put this belief first in our work at Acton Academy; it became our fulcrum.

Later that night, after we said good-bye to Oliver, we pulled yellow notepads from the kitchen drawer and wrote down the heroes of learning who would be our muses.

SOCRATES

Socrates, the ancient Greek teacher and philosopher, taught by asking questions and claimed to know nothing. He inspired youth to seek the truth through relentless questioning. The Socratic method has been proven over the centuries to be the best path on which to hone critical thinking and seek understanding of the human condition beyond simply learning facts.

The key to being successful within this method is more than creating strong questions to provoke students to think. The power lies in a commitment not to answer questions at all. With this commitment comes the understanding from the students that they are in charge of figuring out answers rather than being given them from an expert. The students themselves become teachers and seekers of knowledge and wisdom.

THOMAS JEFFERSON

Our third president, and principal author of the Declaration of Independence, believed in learning by doing. He taught by example; he believed in the value of apprenticeships and mentors.

"Do you want to know who you are?" he asked. "Don't ask. Act! Action will delineate and define you."

In our approach, students would seek a new apprenticeship each year of their middle school and high school journeys in areas of their greatest curiosity. This would begin with personal inventories to pinpoint interests and potential passions. Then, they would research opportunities and create a list of people to contact. The students would learn how to write an email that would be answered, secure an interview, and finally practice how to master the interview itself. Then, they would do the real-world work, spending 40–160 hours of their school year working at the knees of a master in the field.

MARIA MONTESSORI

Maria Montessori was a doctor and innovative educator in the first half of the twentieth century. She developed a schooling philosophy based on student self-direction that is in use across the world today. The main tenets of her method are mixed-age classrooms for peer teaching, with emphases on hands-on and self-paced learning experiences. The adult guide's major role is to set up the environment properly, with expectations and boundaries that enable the children to take charge of their learning rather than wait to be told what to do.

SUGATA MITRA

Sugata Mitra may have captured our thinking the most, as he knew the power of technology and how it freed children to learn without an adult teacher standing in front of them to deliver knowledge. He trusted children with big questions and knew their curiosity would rule the day. He also knew young people could lead and manage each other.

Jeff had met Dr. Mitra at a gathering of the John Templeton Foundation to honor philanthropic innovators. Although his PhD is in physics, Dr. Mitra is most recognized for his inventions and innovations in the fields of cognitive science and education technology.

His stories of children in the slums of Calcutta learning without adult supervision are surprising, yet they made so much sense to us. He simply set up a computer kiosk in a village and left it alone for the children to play with freely. He had cameras so he could watch what happened.

Within hours, the children had figured out how to use the computer and had hacked into the Disney website, even after being blocked. After a few weeks, these kids were clambering over each other to use the computer. It was chaotic until a twelve-year-old girl took over and organized the group. Soon, they were learning everything from DNA replication to the English language—with no adults in charge.

Dr. Mitra coined the term *minimally invasive education* and continues these experiments today.

"Minimally invasive education—that's what I want for our children," I told Jeff, "so they can be free and joyful in their discoveries while working on things that matter to them.

"And I want to be courageous enough to let them fall into chaos until one of the other children steps up to lead. I want to be as strong as Sugata Mitra."

I knew I had a way to go on that one.

SAL KHAN

Sal Khan became an early mentor as we formed Acton Academy. We met him at an education conference when Khan was making headlines with his free online videos teaching math concepts (called Khan Academy). We bonded quickly over our shared belief that given the right tools, children could drive their own education. Soon after that meeting, the three of us shared ideas on the phone. After we hung up, Jeff summed up the data available for online assessment perfectly: "Never in the history of time has more information been available for parents to see how their child is doing in math. I'm just glad I'm not a math teacher, with Khan Academy taking over."

SAM, CHARLIE, AND TAITE SANDEFER

We knew that it was our children who would teach us the most about learning. They already had as we watched them learn to talk, walk, read, write, build, sell, create, persuade, and plan, all without an expert teaching them. They would also be the ones to give us feedback—quickly and more honestly than anyone in the universe. And they'd be our guinea pigs as we tested projects, schedules, and programs.

Ramping up our bandwidth: technology and learning

We found ourselves in an auspicious time in the history of education for such work. Technology was changing everything. The wave of online learning was building so much momentum that it felt like a tsunami hitting the old bastion of tradition. Though the wave had been growing slowly for decades, by the end of 2009, millions of American students in K–12 schools were engaged in some kind of online learning. Technology was freeing up access to learning and lowering costs of delivery.

We saw the impact at home with our young children, too. They were using online games to learn everything from math to entrepreneurship to civil engineering. Technology was making my children into independent seekers of learning—with very little need for me to guide them. It seemed natural and intuitive to them. This spoke volumes about the opportunity that awaited all methods of schooling.

But there was still fear and skepticism from parents, as there always is when new technology enters our lives. Even Wilbur and Orville Wright faced flak when they made bicycles more readily available to children: Wouldn't those bicycles take children far away from home, to places where danger lurked?

We knew we'd be battling such concerns by providing laptops and Internet access to each of our students; but the quality of online learning programs and the numbers of users kept growing exponentially. There was no turning back. It was time to embrace the Internet for what it was worth. And we saw lots of worth.

We also saw the risks and problems we'd need to solve. We knew the children would use computers for only about a quarter of their work time, but could we free parents from the fear their kids would be glued to a screen all day? What safeguards could we install so inappropriate material wouldn't pop up? What laptops would be most economical and user-friendly? Could instruction on the Internet truly replace real, live teachers? How should we test for quality in content and delivery?

We had many questions but were ready to test and experiment until we found the best online programs for children available. This was one tsunami we were going to ride.

I look back on the day Jeff came home that afternoon telling me "we are done" with traditional school and wonder what would have happened if I'd had a crystal ball. If I could have seen the challenges that lay ahead, would I still have said yes to this journey? On that day, the decision was clear and simple. Of course we could create our own school for our children.

I had no idea what I was getting myself into.

CHAPTER 3

BECOMING REAL—
First a Fair, Then a School

"There is not another school on the face of the Earth where
we'd rather our daughter go. It's truly mind-boggling good fortune,
and we owe it all to you and Jeff."

—JAMIE JONES AND AI FJANDRA FERNANDEZ, ACTON ACADEMY PARENTS

The Children's Business Fair

Twelve white-peaked tents sat in a row on our front lawn, and each tent contained a six-foot table and two folding chairs. It was our inaugural Children's Business Fair, October 2007. Sam's idea was coming to life. Little did we know the prototype for our school was about to become a reality. This fair was our vision of how children should learn, and it was being born.

Our young entrepreneurs arrived before the sun came up. Sam was selling hot chocolate, Charlie was selling his homemade dog biscuits, and Taite had her mysteriously delicious chocolate-chip cookie treats packaged and ready. The other children emptied boxes and bags full of homemade products on their tables— jewelry, stationery, swords, painted rocks, and hand-painted

T-shirts. They unloaded small cash boxes and handcrafted banners and tablecloths to complete the setup of their individual booths—their very own small businesses.

Ranging from four to ten years old, these children hailed from public and private schools, along with a couple of homeschoolers, all from Austin, Texas. Our application to participate required them to write a business plan, including start-up costs, pricing, and projected revenue. More important, it specified that each business was to be purely driven by the child—*no parents were allowed to help*. They'd keep the profit as well, minus a $10 booth fee. The children signed a contract stating that if they had to borrow money from their parents, they would pay them back from their proceeds.

Hundreds of people streamed into our yard to check out this little fair. Our flyers had done the trick. People were buying products, and children were haggling, calculating, smiling, and working really hard.

By noon, we had learned two important things. First, children can do far more than we imagined. Second, parents have a very hard time stepping back when there is a possibility that their children might fail or even simply be uncomfortable. But they felt success, too, as they watched their children beaming.

"It worked!" Sam said, who had sold out of his hot chocolate quickly. Charlie and Taite were too busy counting their revenue to look up and acknowledge Sam's excitement.

This first fair was our introduction of Acton Academy to the world. As the customers meandered through the booths and spoke with the children, word had spread that we were starting a school based on the principles of this fair. Hands-on learning. Children leading themselves. Real-world problem solving.

The Children's Business Fair was a true experiment, with no grand plan but for our own children to have a fun learning experience and practice some entrepreneurial skills. Our initial approach to the school was much the same. We pulled together ideas and strategies until we found the ones that worked best.

Keeping Austin Weird

At the same time that we were launching our first Children's Business Fair, Austin was becoming one of America's hot spots. For decades it had been a town built on state government, live music, and academia, all strung around the University of Texas.

Starting in the late 1980s through the turn of the century, Austin began attracting innovative industries, including technology, gaming, and filmmaking. By 2007, we were surrounded by creative genius and hot conversations about disruption in education through the advent of online learning. This—along with the burgeoning homeschooling population, alternative school options, and the rising cost of a college degree with no guarantee of a job afterward—was sparking questions about traditional schooling.

Although what we were thinking of doing seemed crazy to some, we were in the right place at the right time to begin something radical. "Keep Austin Weird" is our town motto, and we fit right in.

Now nearly a decade later, Acton Children's Business Fairs, like Acton Academy, have expanded across the country, in particular in cities like Detroit, where they're led by strong moms and community leaders wanting to give their children a chance to become entrepreneurs. Each one still reflects the most important ingredients for a thriving Acton Academy—children on a mission, with clear boundaries, great freedom, and responsibility. And a chance to show the world what they can *do*.

But we didn't pay much attention to the fair. We had a school to launch.

Finding a home for Acton Academy

After six months of looking for an initial location, we saw a For Lease sign on a property about two miles from our house. It was love at first sight—a small, charming home with wooden floors that had been converted into an architect's office, close to downtown.

Our sweet little building did not have a yard, but it was within walking distance of a park. The tiny parking area out the back door became our "field." We could paint a Four-Square court, pull in a mobile basketball hoop, and stick a ping-pong table under the carport.

I now had something I could dig my hands into. I was driven to create a home more than a school. I wanted it to smell good when you walked in the door—bread-baking-in-the-oven kind of good. And warm lights, not fluorescent. I wanted windows without blinds and living plants we could feed and watch grow. I wanted soft, inviting textures in pillows and rugs. I veered away from bulletin boards with preprinted happy faces and apples. I wanted the children's words and ideas painted on the walls with their own hands. I wanted our space to feed our sense of intimacy and trust. I wanted it to be a place that lingered in their minds as they left each day. Place matters.

One afternoon I walked my friend Carolyn Robinson through our little school. As we were closing the door behind us, she said, "How do we sign up? We've been hoping you and Jeff would start a school!"

Her son, Cash, was in Charlie's Montessori class. He and Charlie had become bonded over the Hank the Cowdog book series. She and her husband, Rhett, had been looking for a small, hands-on learning experience for Cash, since our Montessori school didn't have an upper-elementary program. She knew us well and trusted that what we would build for our own children would suit Cash just fine.

Her trust was humbling to me—and a breath of encouragement that kept me strong as I was taking my steps into the unknown.

Hiring our first guide

At this point we were a small, merry band—not a school.

We were missing one vital piece of our quickly evolving plan—a teacher. I knew it was critical for us to find the right one if we wanted to attract more families.

Even though our ultimate vision was to have no teachers, only guides, we knew the credentials of a Montessori teacher would bring expertise in the area of setting up the environment and communicating with parents about the psychology of learning. A master Montessori teacher would help us build a culture and a community. As time went on, we would train this person to use the Socratic method and change the title from "teacher" to "guide."

Kaylie Dienelt had been Charlie and Cash's teacher at the Montessori school. She was smart, creative, entrepreneurial, and worldly. She was fascinated with children and learning and the psychology behind it. She had been on my mind as the perfect teacher for Acton Academy, but I didn't have the heart to pluck her from a school she seemed to be thriving in. As luck would have it, she had just notified the school that she'd be leaving.

I called her immediately. "What are your plans regarding teaching?" I asked.

"I have heard through the grapevine about your school idea and am intrigued. I'd love to talk with you about it."

I knew as I hung up the phone we'd found our future master guide.

Recruiting fellow travelers

We had core beliefs, a location, a guide—and only three students, two of whom were our own sons. Who would join us? I placed an advertisement in a local parenting magazine:

ACTON ACADEMY. WHERE EVERY
CHILD BEGINS A HERO'S JOURNEY.

Do you believe character matters more than tests? And free play is more important than homework? Do you

yearn for your child to find a calling and not just a career?
Join us at our open house to learn more.

Our open house was scheduled to run from 8:00 a.m. to
5:00 p.m. for five straight days. On the first day, I sat alone. Waiting. The clock ticked. Warm sun streamed through the window
and brightened the front rooms. And then it happened. The
front door of Acton Academy opened.

As the first couple walked in, I stuck out my hand, probably a
little too eagerly. "Welcome to Acton Academy!" I said.

The man, tall and dark with kind eyes, was wearing a yellow
button-down shirt tucked into his jeans. He wore the same work
boots that the contractor who built our home wore. "Hi, Laura,"
he said. "I'm Divit—and this is Becca. We saw your advertisement and came to learn more about your school for our son,
Bodhi."

"Thanks so much for coming," I said. "Our first day of school
will be Tuesday, September 2. We plan to start very small and
grow slowly. Our goal is seven to nine students for the first year.

"Let's walk through the space, so I can describe our philosophy of learning and what we'll be doing here every day."

Thus began the first tour. Three weeks later, Bodhi was one of
the seven students secured for our first year.

We had a school. Now we needed to deliver on our promises.

CHAPTER 4

CROSSING *the* THRESHOLD—
Time to Start School

"In no uncertain terms, Chelsea and I are GRATEFUL every day that you and Jeff decided to dedicate a large portion of your lives to a better education for children around the world. The organic but purposeful development of our daughter's thoughts, speech, curiosity, confidence, empathy, joy, kindness, courage, tenacity, vulnerability, problem-solving skills, AND academics are mind-blowing to us on a daily basis."

—DAVID KING, ACTON ACADEMY PARENT

It was late August 2009, only days before Acton Academy's first day of school. We were sitting in our living room, sharing a cup of coffee with Jamie Wheal, a leading expert on the neural physiology of high-performance athletics and creativity. He and his wife, Julie, were homeschooling their seven-year-old daughter and nine-year-old son.

We had asked him to join us in a discussion about the basic question: How do we choreograph the experience of the first days at Acton so the students gain a sense of purpose?

"Help us so we don't miss something important," I said.

"Never forget the power of ceremony," Jamie said. "Resist falling into the administrative abyss of making dreaded announcements when you gather your families together. Do the opposite. Don't ever make an administrative announcement. Inspire the parents each time you call them together with a commitment to the ideals and promises of Acton Academy—excellence, hard work, kindness, responsibility, and freedom. And the fact that each child has genius within."

In that moment, Jeff and I vowed we would never stand up in front of the Acton parents and make announcements about parking or lunches or calendars or rules or attendance. All of that could be documented in something they could read on their own or learn from their child. Our school gatherings would be times for reflection, growth, and inspiration. We would honor the time, intelligence, and spirits of our Acton Academy community members. This was the bow we tied around our plan of action, and we thanked Jamie heartily as we walked him to his car.

I sat down that evening and wrote an email to the Acton parents:

Dear Founding Families,

Your journey is about to begin.

On Tuesday, September 2, at 8 a.m. you will drop your child off at the back gate of Acton Academy for our very first, first day of school. All they need to bring with them is lunch and a couple of snacks for the day. They are welcome to bring a book from home if they are reading one at the moment. We'll have everything they need—no need to buy any school supplies.

Before that momentous occasion, though, we invite you to join us for our **Founding Family Ceremony** next Thursday, August 28, at 10 a.m. at Acton Academy. Together we will begin an adventure of a lifetime. See you then.

With excitement,

Laura

Ceremony first

On that Thursday, at 9:45 a.m., each new Acton student and parent was standing on the front porch of Acton Academy awaiting our Founding Family Ceremony

Charlie and Sam stood outside too. We were going to treat them not like the owners' children but as our special guests, our valued stakeholders. We wanted them to feel, when they walked into the room, just as welcomed, nervous, and excited as the other new students felt.

Our boys knew two of the other new families, both from their Montessori school. Cash Robinson, seven, had been in Charlie's class; Chris Carpenter, six, had been in Sam's. Chris's older sister, Ellie, stood tall and quiet next to her parents. At nine, she was the oldest in the group. Bodhi was there, too; he was tracing cracks in the sidewalk with a stick he had found. And Saskia, at age five, was our youngest student. She stood bravely with her parents. These were the people who had filled out our application, paid their deposits, and signed the parent contract. But more important, these were the first brave souls to trust us with the education of their children—and trust their children to take ownership of their journey. These were our founding families.

. . .

I walked out and welcomed each person to come inside.

Jeff and I had decided on our roles for leading the school early on in our planning. I would be the head of school, running daily operations, quality control, and working with the guides, parents, and students to create a tight community. Jeff was still teaching at the Acton School of Business and running his energy investment firm. He couldn't be a presence at the school often but would be the brains behind developing the curriculum, would advise me on growth and finances, and would be our master of ceremonies for community gatherings.

This was the first of his ceremonial launches, and the excitement in the room was electric. Jeff has a special gift for moving an audience; I was as drawn in as the children. He walked to the front of the room and motioned the group to gather around him. All became silent.

"Today is a day about making a choice. You've all signed up to be here, but now the deep, heartfelt decision must be made.

"I'd like to share a story with you that my friend Oliver DeMille shared with me.

"The year is 1764. A student named Thomas Jefferson is dumped by his girlfriend, who immediately marries his best friend. This event is so devastating that twenty years later, he is still writing about it in his journal. Jefferson decides to give up on romance and rededicate himself to his studies.

"In that same year, 1764, John Adams is a teacher. He writes in his journal that he enjoys teaching because it allows him to escape the frustrating worlds of business and politics and gives him a chance to think and learn. Later that year, he will meet and marry another thinker and writer, Abigail.

"That same year, James Madison is thirteen years old. He is a good student, but so quiet and shy that his parents wonder if he will ever amount to much.

"In 1764, George Washington is a businessman. His journal shows that his top priority that year is to pay off his debts, to which he has foolishly given a personal guarantee.

"A decade later, this same group of ordinary people will declare independence from the greatest power on the face of the earth and sign it with their lives, fortunes, and sacred honor.

"A decade after that, they will write and help ratify the United States Constitution. But in 1764, they are just ordinary people, like us."

The parents were hanging on every word, but Jeff was clearly speaking more to the children. They had gathered and sat by his feet and he squatted down to be on eye level with them.

"There comes a time when ordinary people like us have to choose. Acton Academy is a choice. It is a choice to begin a Hero's Journey—an adventure that is fun and exciting but also includes falling down, making mistakes, failing. People on such a journey are heroes not because they have superpowers but because they choose to get back up after falling down. And they help their fellow travelers do the same. At Acton, you will have mentors and guides. But each of you will be in charge of your own journey.

"Look behind me. We have drawn a line on the floor. It symbolizes the choice we are all making. Where we are now symbolizes the ordinary world. Across that line is new territory. It is where your Hero's Journey will begin. We are going to ask each family to make sure you are ready to cross the line into your new life as the founding families of Acton Academy. Are you ready to make a choice?"

After Jeff finished speaking, he stood up and stepped back.

One by one, I called each family's name. I asked them if they were ready to choose this journey called Acton Academy. "If so, please hold hands and walk together over the line into uncharted territory."

As each family crossed into the next room, spontaneous applause broke out. We were all in. We were Acton Academy.

To close the ceremony, we all signed a copy of the Acton Promises (see appendix A). Kaylie then led the children to the back room. She dipped a brush into a bucket of red paint and asked Chris to come forward. After making sure Chris was okay with having his hand painted, Kaylie colored his palm and said, "Find a place to put your handprint on the wall. Then take a pen and sign your name." She continued with a different color of paint for each child. The children then called their parents over and took charge of painting their palms, printing them on the wall, and having them sign their names.

Each of us had said yes to the Acton Hero's Journey; we had claimed this space as our own.

And we're off!

On the first day of school, our second guide would join us. Anna Blabey hailed from a background of outdoor education and project development. She, like Kaylie, had traveled the world and was ready to learn the Socratic method and witness children taking charge of their learning.

As the guides waited for the students' arrival inside the schoolhouse, I waited in the parking lot. This would become my daily routine—to greet each child as they arrived. The family cars began pulling in. Our agreement with parents was for them to say good-bye to their child in the car and let the children enter their new school on their own. This was the children's special place. Adults were not the central figures here—the children were. Marking this as the first day of school and a new life journey, I handed each parent a yellow rose and said, "Thank you for trusting us with your children. See you at 3:15."

I watched each young hero walk alone up the back stairs into Acton Academy. These steps were their first achievement on their journeys. They were walking alone into territory where no other children had gone. Whether they fully understood it or not, they were the pioneers of student-driven learning. Their choices each day would carve a path for others to follow.

The schedule for the day was posted on the refrigerator and in each room (see chart on page 52).

8:00–8:25	Free time
8:25–8:45	Morning Launch discussion: Meet in a circle on the green rug
8:45–9:00	Team-building activity: Meet in the back play area
9:00–11:00	Core skills time: Reading or online math—your choice
11:00–11:15	Clean up and organize work
11:15–11:30	Group discussion: Reflecting on your work
11:30–12:00	Lunch
12:00–12:15	Lunch cleanup
12:15–12:45	Free time—No tech
12:45–2:45	Project Time: Entrepreneurship
2:45–3:00	Studio maintenance
3:00–3:15	Closing group

Note: PE and art will be on Tuesdays and Thursdays from 8:30am–10:30am.

Our goal was for the children to have everything they needed within their space, so they knew what to do and when to do it without needing an adult to make announcements, answer questions, or give directions. Maria Montessori was so right. If the adult designs and sets up the environment with the children's line of sight in mind, the children can function independently and happily.

By 8:25 a.m., every student was sitting quietly on the green rug, which they would soon name "the artichoke rug."

First things first—push power to the children

"Welcome to Acton Academy," Ms. Kaylie said, using the familiar title we chose to use for our guides. "Let's start our day with a greeting. I'll show you first by greeting Ms. Anna, and then you do it with each other."

She turned to Ms. Anna, who was sitting on her left, looked her in the eyes, shook her hand, and said, "Good morning, Ms. Anna." She then looked to her right, and there sat Ellie.

Ellie looked Kaylie in the eyes, shook her hand, and said, "Good morning, Ms. Kaylie."

The children caught on immediately and took over. A nice buzz of movement and words rose up as the group of young pioneers started their first day of Acton Academy acknowledging each other formally.

We've performed this small ceremony every morning for eight years. With a simple greeting, each student is known, seen, and called by name. And simple ceremony binds people together.

Doing the same thing at the same time every day. This builds intimacy, the first step in building a space for learning.

"Part of learning about yourself is knowing when you need fuel and hydration," Kaylie said. "When do you most need fuel—in the morning before you get to work or after you play?" This discussion led to a wide-open sharing. It was clear that each child had a different idea about when he or she would need a snack. It may seem mundane, talking about food as the first group discussion. But thinking more deeply, isn't food the bonding force of a tribe, and doesn't talking about it give each person something to say? Our goal for this precious first moment was to level the playing field in a mixed-age group where there were varying levels of knowledge and skill sets. Everyone has an opinion about food.

"You get to choose when you have your snacks or water breaks. No need to ask permission. You are in charge."

Not only did this discussion break the ice during a time that was probably stressful for everyone, but the conclusion of it gave the group of children a sense of power and freedom. The message meant so much—we trust you and you have power. You don't need to ask us to get a drink or have a snack. And by all means, when you have to go to the bathroom, please do so; you know where it is.

Connecting the learners to each other

Anna's background in outdoor education gave her the skills to create engaging team-building experiences. She designed the first days of school to allow the group to bond and gain basic collaborative and communication skills with short, interactive games aimed to inspire laughter and a mini crisis of frustration—two of life's great bonding experiences.

"Join me outside," she said to the children. As they walked to the parking lot-turned-mini-playground, they saw the bright blue plastic tarp she had laid out. It was just small enough to make it hard for everyone to fit on it. "Everyone please stand on the tarp. At least one foot must be on the tarp for the duration of singing 'Row, Row, Row Your Boat.' No other part of your bodies can touch the ground." They finished the song. She said, "Now we will fold the tarp in half and do it again. We are going to see how small we can make this tarp and still have each of you touching it with one foot for the full singing of the song." The group fell into a heap after the fourth folding of the tarp.

Anna then asked them to sit in a circle and asked them questions. Did anyone think it would be impossible to fit the entire group on the smallest tarp? What made it possible? How many of you got frustrated? Did you have to change strategies? When else in life have you faced an impossible task and become frustrated? What did you do? For twenty minutes, this group of young children shared their feelings of frustration and success. They listened to each other. They were becoming a group.

Work and play every day

The day continued with other purposeful activities: quiet reading time with a book of each person's choice; practicing the online math programs to decide which one worked best for each child; writing in personal journals; lunch; free time; and project time with challenges to create products to sell to each other, bargain, trade, and calculate value. This was the beginning of our first entrepreneurship project. Anna set up a supplies store where students could purchase what they needed to create their projects and gave each student $5 to spend or save. Hard, messy, collaborative work, with real engagement and measurable outcome. Project time ended with "studio maintenance"—cleanup time.

Then, the day ended where it started—everyone sitting in a circle together.

Closing the day with seeds and Socrates

This time when they gathered at the green rug, the students found a large bowl filled with green, red, pink, and yellow apples in the center of a circle, alongside a knife and a cutting board.

Kaylie began by picking up the bowl and holding it on her lap. The students eagerly sat down, folding their legs in front of them. She took one apple at a time out of the bowl, turned it around in her hand, and looked at it intently. She then passed the first one to Bodhi, who was sitting on her left.

"As you take the apple," Kaylie said, "look at it closely. Really analyze its appearance—the skin, stem, color, texture—and then pass it to the person next to you. Keep passing them around as you receive and analyze them."

After the apples had gone around, Kaylie put them back in the bowl and said, "Did the apples look the same?"

"Not at all," Bodhi said.

"How were they different? You can call on each other rather than raising your hand to speak. Bodhi, you can continue with your thoughts and then call on someone else."

"Some had bruises; others didn't," he said and then nodded to Charlie to speak. They took turns sharing, calling on each other as they went.

"One had a really long stem."

"None of them were the same color."

"The shapes were really different. Some were small; some were big. Some were round, but others were more oval-shaped."

"Now, let's see what they look like on the inside," Kaylie said. She took each apple and cut it in half across the middle, then passed the halves around. The students were quiet except for a few "oohs" and "aahs."

"Ellie, what do you see?" she asked.

"Each one has a star of seeds inside. They all look exactly the same on the inside."

"The seeds of potential," Kaylie said. "It's like each of you: so different on the outside, but inside, you have a star. You, too, have seeds of potential. Do the seeds in these apples automatically become apple trees?"

"Not if you throw them away," said Cash. "You have to plant them if you want them to grow."

"But not just plant them," said Chris. "You have to water them and make sure they have sunshine."

"These are like your seeds of potential," Kaylie said. "Everyone has them. We call this your *genius*—your potential for greatness that is unique to you. But if you don't nurture the seeds of potential inside you and help them grow, they'll die and waste away, just like apple seeds tossed into the trash." She paused to let this settle in, and then asked, "How can we help each other's seeds of potential grow? How can we be the good soil, water, and sun to ourselves and each other?"

Ms. Anna grabbed a whiteboard to record their ideas:

- Read good books.

- Don't bother people when they are working.

- Say nice words. Don't say "stupid."

- Be curious.

- Work hard.

- Practice.

- Tell the truth.

This was the Socratic method in action—a guide asking questions and moving deeper with the children's responses, all the while holding tightly to the boundaries of time and discussion rules.

Kaylie looked at the clock and knew she had to close the day.

"Let's keep this list and think more about how we can help each other grow our seeds of potential. Next week, we are going to write our contract. This will include the promises we make to each other."

Kaylie explained the importance of keeping promises, of honoring the contract, and what type of consequences there might be for breaking the promises. Then she closed for the day.

"Thank you for a wonderful day of learning. *Namaste*. The light in me honors the light in you."

Kaylie and Anna were adding their own personal touch to the ceremonial feel of Acton. "Namaste" was Kaylie's gentle kindness shining through.

"Namaste," the students said in unison.

Little did we know on that day that the gracious Hindu expression would become the traditional closing of every single day at Acton Academy. The traditions were beginning.

CHAPTER 5

LEARN BY DOING—
Wrestling with Rebels and Rulers

"A couple of days ago Nicholas was getting ready for school and
tears were streaming down his cheeks because his sunburn hurt
so badly. I was ready to have him stay home, work from his laptop,
and apply more aloe every hour. When he realized this was my
plan he said, 'Wait! I can't stay home! I've got work to do!'
Even a year ago, I would have never imagined him exhibiting that level
of responsibility. I wouldn't have dreamed it was possible. I'm glad he
learned the lessons that lead to responsibility in sixth grade instead
of during his freshman year of college."

—ROBERT YACKTMAN, ACTON ACADEMY PARENT

As our first year continued, each learner was coming into his
or her own sense of self in our space. I was witnessing a tribe of
strong personalities forging its customs. From soft-spoken and
shy to rambunctious and active, each child's individuality shone
through while being tempered to fuel the covenant-bound group.

When one spoke too softly in a group discussion, another
would say, "We can't hear what you said and we want to hear it.
Could you please say it a little louder?" When one child pushed

another at the drinking fountain, another would say, "We don't do that at Acton." When one took more cookies than the allotted amount during lunch, someone was bound to say, "That's not okay." And when one was making too much noise during reading time, it never took more than a few seconds before I'd witness another redirecting him to his book.

These young students were sticklers for their standards, and they had set them very high with their Student Contract (*see* Appendix B). They were not afraid to claim their new role in life as managers of their space and time. The children were gentle and consistent in their feedback to each other.

This became the foundational practice for peer accountability. The adults were easily released from the role of classroom managers or disciplinarians. Each student strayed from the rules at times in minor ways. But not one disagreed with the premise that the rules were legitimate and the contract was sacred. They were the authors of both, and they took pride in their identity as the Acton Academy community. This was their culture.

This group of seven children set the path for our future by finding their voices with each other. The words were clear and kindly spoken. And they were heard. Together, the students would be the ones to carry this torch forward. The roots of a student-driven community were taking hold.

Hark! A messenger!

On a cool November morning, the children were focused on their independent core skills work. The excitement of the new school year had settled into a comfortable routine. The Entrepreneurship Quest was a big success, culminating in the Second Annual Children's Business Fair, which had more than tripled in size. The Contract was signed and hanging on the wall. The seven founding students were now a group of intentional learners on a mission. There was a relaxed, quiet buzz around the schoolhouse.

Suddenly, there was knocking at the front door. Ms. Kaylie called everyone together. This was not a normal thing for her to do. She declared that the king wasn't happy that we had our own free school.

"He has his eye on us and will be sending us a letter soon," she said. "I think this is his messenger coming to the door now."

Ms. Anna was standing outside. She had on a black tricorne hat with a faux white ponytail hanging down the back. Her jeans were tucked into black boots, and her white shirt was buttoned up high under her blue blazer.

"I deliver to you on behalf of King George this proclamation," she announced. "You are under the order of the king to follow it."

She handed Kaylie the proclamation, which was rolled up and tied with a ribbon. Kaylie unrolled it and read it out loud.

"King George has ordered each person to take everything out of your desk and stack it on the right corner. From now on, nothing may be put in your desk. Everything must be stacked on top."

The students giggled. This was fun. It was a game and they knew it. They ran to their desks and did as they were ordered.

For the rest of the day, every thirty minutes, a proclamation would be delivered and read out loud. Each one was hung on the wall above the fireplace.

You must ask permission to go to the bathroom.

Snack time will be only at 10 a.m. and 2 p.m. No one can choose any other time, and all snacks must be eaten in the kitchen.

Everyone must line up at the door and walk outside together for free time.

You are allowed to do only math work this morning. No reading or writing.

You are allowed to read only the books on this list.

The fun lasted for the first few announcements. Then the students began to get annoyed. The day closed with more than a couple of frowns and grumbles.

The king's injustice

The students returned the next morning expecting the start of what they considered to be a normal day. It was not.

There were more proclamations, more restrictions, more alterations to the routine. By midday, when they realized they were not getting much work done, their annoyance turned to anger and tears. Their freedoms were gone. They were being directed, lectured to, and strictly monitored.

"This isn't fair," Bodhi said.

"We can't work under these circumstances," Charlie said, seriously upset with this change of fate.

"We deserve to be able to eat when we need to and go to the bathroom when we need to," another voice added.

"This isn't Acton anymore."

A revolt and a roll of the die

Anna waited for silence, then said, "If you believe a revolution against King George is the only way for you to get back on track with your learning, you may choose to revolt." She paused. "But there is a high probability of losing.

"If you choose to revolt, you must write a formal declaration of independence," she explained. "And then you must roll the die. If you roll a one or two, you win. Three, four, five, or six and you lose. Losing is significant. It means you will lose free play time and dessert at lunch for the rest of the session—four more weeks."

Stern and tight-lipped, Ms. Anna played the part perfectly. The students' anger only increased. We had not fixed the die. This was a real-life experience in learning how to calculate odds and weigh risk, with real consequences.

Charlie took the lead.

"Revolt!" he cried out. "I'll start writing our declaration now!"

And so he did. They all gathered around him, and after his

first sentences—*We are not animals! We deserve to learn freely without the intrusion of terrible rules!*—each one added a sentence or two, then signed it with a flourish. Then they stormed up to the wall of proclamations and pinned their declaration of independence on top of them.

"Are you sure you want to do this?" Ms. Kaylie said. "It's very risky."

"Yes, and we've chosen Charlie to roll the die," Ellie said in her quiet, steady voice with confidence.

Kaylie, Anna, and I were anxious. This could turn out terribly. If it didn't work out, there would be lots of tears and some very upset children going home today. And the rest of the session would be more like the traditional school we had rebelled against in the first place. I had to leave the studio—I couldn't watch the rolling of the die. What Jeff and I envisioned as critical learning experiences for our children—real risk taking with the potential of experiencing failure or loss—now felt like a bad idea. Couldn't they just read about the risk those early rebels took in a textbook? We were setting up experiences in which the adults had no idea what the outcome would be.

While this is the essence of the Socratic method, when combined with this level of experiential learning, it was feeling like a real punch in the gut for me—one who likes to control things. I was beginning to sense what the emotional journey of an Acton parent looked like—a personal journey fraught with feeling out of control, anxious, and vulnerable. I stayed in my small office and listened at the doorway.

The guides gathered the group and gave Charlie the die. "Remember, you must roll either a one or a two to gain your freedoms back," Anna said.

"Go, Charlie!" Cash said.

Charlie shook and shook and shook the die. He tossed it. The room was silent except for the die bouncing along the wooden floor. When it stopped, Anna looked at it.

"It's a two!"

Joy and relief. Everyone, including Kaylie and Anna, squealed with glee. The children ran up to the wall of proclamations and started ripping them off with great vigor. When they were all torn off the wall, they looked at each other and said, "We can now do any work we want!"

Within five minutes, they were all moving into places at their desks or on beanbags or at the common tables in the kitchen. Our schoolhouse became peaceful and quiet again. They were free to work. And working is exactly what they wanted. They would have time the next day to reflect on their learning and process the experience with the guides. This would include writing and discussing the knowledge they gained about American history and, more importantly, what freedom means, what it felt like to have it stripped away, and how this experience will impact their lives moving forward.

But for now, it was time to revel in being able to do the work of their choice.

Claiming our identity

We traveled through the days and weeks, as happy sojourners with each day's learning directing us toward the next day. The students had found their strides using the online math programs (see appendix H), were reading and writing every day, managing conflicts based on their Contract, painting an outdoor mural, working their bodies hard in PE, and launching into their next project, robotics and electronics. No one felt the urge to stray from our mission or skirt from working each day. This group of young children showed up early and stayed late. They wanted to be there and they wanted to learn.

By mid-January, it felt like we were missing something. We knew the character traits we valued in each other—courage, curiosity, kindness, responsibility, and good humor. We knew our mission—that each person would find a calling and change the world. We knew what our Contract stated—our essential rules to grow our seeds of potential.

But who were we? We needed an identity, a symbol to show the world. "A mascot!" Ellie said one afternoon. The group started listing their ideas for a mascot on a whiteboard. They decided over lunch one day that the list of potential mascots was long enough—Owls, Eagles, Aviators, Aces, Knights. It was time to discuss the options and then vote. It took their whole free time to finish debating the qualities of the prospective mascots. It was time for a vote.

"Should we let the parents vote?" asked Ms. Anna. All agreed this was a good idea. I sent an email to each family that afternoon so they could discuss and send their votes back to me. That evening the votes rolled in.

I arrived at school the next day with an announcement. It was a tie between Owls and Eagles. We needed to take another vote. Another email home and another evening later, we had our mascot.

We were now the Acton Academy Eagles.

Growing pains

Word gets out quickly in a town when parents and children are having a happy time with their learning experience. With very little advertising or publicity, I began getting daily phone calls for applications and requests for tours. We still felt like we were living in an idyllic world—our sweet schoolhouse with so much learning happening each day—and I was enjoying flying under the radar. More than that, I was afraid of what growth might do to our wonderful learning community.

"Jeff, what if this is working only because we have three particular magical ingredients in place right now—two great guides, seven amazing children, and a perfect setting? I just enrolled another family with two older boys. I'm afraid the whole thing might fall apart."

I was feeling scared and selfish at the same time. Part of me didn't want anyone to know about our little school. The children were thriving. We felt more like a family than a school. And I wasn't the only one who felt this way. "I don't want to tell my friends about this," Carolyn said to me one day as she dropped off Cash. "I want to keep this all to ourselves."

But it was time for Acton to grow.

CHAPTER 6

THE ABYSS *of* ASSESSMENT—

How Do We Prove Learning?

"Why am I happy my kids are at Acton Academy? To boil down
five years of the best, most unexpected gift is like boiling down a
small sea. Our kids have developed confidence to learn independently,
lead with compassion, and develop focus without losing curiosity.
Learning to integrate the balance of freedom and accountability is
having positive impacts in both school and family life."

—YOLANDA KING, ACTON ACADEMY PARENT

As we entered our second year, we had more than doubled in size
and would triple before the year ended. The report Heather Staker
was writing, *The Rise of K–12 Blended Learning*, when she toured
our school had shone the spotlight on Acton Academy. She had
interviewed educators at schools coast-to-coast, from Kentucky to
California, Illinois to New York, Kansas to Florida. Each school
was in some significant way adding digital learning to its curriculum and giving students more leeway in how they used their time

with online tools. *Blended learning* was the term used for this combination of online learning in a bricks-and-mortar school.

"Online learning appears to be a classic disruptive innovation with the potential not just to improve the current model of education delivery," Heather wrote, "but to transform it." Online learning had started small, she continued, with roughly 45,000 K–12 students taking online courses in 2000. "But by 2010," she added, "over 4 million students were participating in some kind of formal online learning program."

She devoted three pages to Acton Academy and gave special attention to "Acton Sims," the series of online simulations Jeff developed to teach entrepreneurship and business finance when he founded the Acton School of Business. They were state-of-the-art interactive experiences for graduate MBA students that we were using with our young learners at Acton Academy.

What seemed to impress Heather—and what separated us from most other blended-learning endeavors—was the role students played in the classroom.

"They are accountable to their peers," she wrote, "and this team-based approach motivates students to master their fundamentals."

Heather Staker's report put Acton on the education map worldwide. On one hand, I could breathe a deep sigh of relief. In 2009 we had embarked on an odyssey with no assurance that our idea of a learning community would work; and less than three years later, an education expert, Heather Staker, had put an academic stamp of approval on our adventure. The report brought credibility and increased interest in Acton Academy.

On the other hand, with added growth we knew our

processes needed to become more systematized. We needed to scale what we were doing to serve a larger group of children and parents.

And we needed to show evidence that real learning was happening.

Test scores: *amazing results but not enough*

We knew we needed a baseline test for two reasons. First, we wanted to make sure nothing was falling through the cracks in terms of core learning—reading, writing, and math. Second, parents want to see how their child compared to peers nationwide.

Over the years we have used the Stanford 10, ERB, and Scantron standardized tests, and most recently moved to the Iowa assessment. All tests proved what we had hoped—the children were progressing easily through more than one grade level per year.

In fact, they were progressing, on average, 3.5 grade levels every nine months. We've even had an Eagle earn a perfect score on the PSAT.

But we wanted to move away from depending on test scores or getting too excited by them.

How could we prove the grander and deeper learning we knew was going on, without reverting to a teacher-driven model that consisted of a teacher delivering information to be memorized and then regurgitated on a test that led to a grade?

In a student-driven environment, can the children prove their progress in a way that makes sense to parents and, ultimately, college admissions officers? Will parents accept proof of their child's learning without needing to see a teacher's final mark on it?

We were about to find out.

Exhibitions of learning: showing what you have learned

We began thinking about what we learned from Sam, Charlie, and Taite.

How did we know when they had learned to walk? They walked! How did we know they could add and subtract in their heads? We'd play the card game 21 with them. Or we'd go to the grocery store and they'd have to shop with a budget. For writing? We could see a comparison of the notes and stories they had written to us over time.

This is the kind of proof we wanted in our community—applying learning to real-world problems to show what the children could *do*. We'd visited High Tech High in San Diego and seen powerful public exhibitions of their students' projects. We'd also seen how the Children's Business Fair played out as the perfect prototype of assessment. Did you make a profit? Could you do the math in your head to give correct change? Were your customers satisfied? Did you create signs and advertisements that were legible and had meaning? What will you do differently next year?

We designed our Exhibitions of Learning to take place every five to six weeks as the Eagles' chance to demonstrate what they had learned over that time period. We'd invite parents and friends to attend and participate in the evaluation of learning.

Examples of exhibitions we held in our first three years included—

- A play written, marketed, produced, and performed on a famous historical stage in downtown Austin. Test? The students, ages six to ten years old, passed out a survey at the end and asked the audience members to share whether or not the play inspired them to find their own calling. They also sat on the edge of the stage after their performance to answer questions about the process and their learning.

- A writers' café with children arranging the room, creating a printed program, welcoming guests, serving lemonade, and then reading their poetry aloud to a community audience. Test? The Eagles had to pitch their piece to a group of peers. Their peers then voted. The winners read out loud. All the poems were included in a printed anthology.

- An art exhibit. Test? A completed, matted, and framed self-portrait. Eagles stood by their works and explained the process of creating their self-portraits and what they had learned.

- A physics competition of simple machines, with the winning team getting its design built into a life-size playground addition. Test? The teams had to pitch their machines to parents, who then voted on which was best designed to be added to the campus playground.

In addition to showing to parents by *doing* what they had

learned, these exhibitions were designed to serve as incentives for the Eagles. Nothing like a deadline and an audience to get people cranking on their work!

But we still weren't satisfied. Test scores and exhibitions couldn't fully capture and celebrate the work and progress happening daily in the studios. More evidence was available and so more evidence could be provided—the work itself.

Portfolios: curating excellent work

We had more data at our fingertips about each Eagle's daily work than I'd ever had when I was going to school. The online learning platforms gave rich details in user-friendly reports for parents and students to analyze. In math, for example, parents could see how much time their child spent on each problem and how many skills had been mastered in a particular topic.

We would give parents the passwords for their children's programs so they could log on and see at any given time how their child was progressing in grammar, math, and reading. Though less familiar than being handed a report card, the data would be rich for any parent who would dig into it.

In addition to the data from their online work, Eagles would cull best samples of writing, art, and project documentation they'd curated over the weeks and put them into a portfolio for their parents to review. Sitting together with the guide in a "portfolio review meeting," parents could ask their child questions and discuss areas of weakness and strength together. Over time, parents would be able to compare a large body of work and see improvements or challenges. Parents wouldn't need to depend on a teacher to tell them whether their child was learning anything. They could see it and assess it for themselves.

And yet . . . it still wasn't enough. Clearly, our model of learning was reaching far beyond merely "learning to know." The bulk of daily life in the studios could be called "learning to do" and "learning to be"—applying knowledge not only to accomplish tasks and solve problems but to be a friend, respect a fellow traveler, recover from a failure, gain confidence, speak in a group with clarity, and rise up to responsibility. How do you assess how a person is progressing in the quest to become more fully human and more completely themselves?

Learning to be: experiences to grow a heart and soul

We had seen how the deep dives into experiential learning— notably in history and science—triggered emotion, problem solving, engagement, and learning in the students, as they had to imagine standing in the shoes of others and make difficult decisions. We knew this would be the meat of our endeavor to create curriculum to help young people "learn how to be."

A clear example of this was the way they came up with their own declaration of independence after having their freedoms stripped away. No textbook could have delivered the same learning about different forms of government, taxation, probabilities, standing up for one's rights, or reasons why people fought for freedom.

While it's risky to let children play out such challenging experiences, we didn't want to do anything less. We built in lots of time for reflection and processing in order to make these experiences lasting and valuable.

And our second year's learning plan felt even riskier than the first. The goal was to understand what discrimination is, prove it still exists, and see if the children were capable of treating classmates differently based on color—in this case, eye color. The test would be the experience itself and the group discussion and personal reflection upon its conclusion.

Jeff had discovered the exercise and knew it was right for Acton Academy. "Our students can handle this," Jeff said.

It was a tough one, I explained. We'll have to be sure the parents are informed before we move forward. This will cause some tears but some great learning, too. "These kids will surprise us," he assured me.

The lesson came from renowned educator Jane Elliott, who years ago put her third-grade class through a now-famous program that became known as the "Blue Eyes/Brown Eyes" exercise.

For two days, she divided her class by eye color. On the first day, the blue-eyed people were "on top." They got more free time, were able to get second helpings at lunch, and could use the water fountain. The brown-eyed students had to wear large blue collars "so the blue-eyed students could tell who they were from far away." They were forced to stay inside for free time, had to use small paper cups instead of the water fountain, and got only one serving of lunch.

On the second day they switched, and the "brown-eyes were on top."

Elliott came up with her exercise in 1968, after the assassination of Dr. Martin Luther King Jr. "The shooting of Martin Luther King could not just be talked about or explained away," Elliott said in the PBS *Frontline* documentary *A Class Divided*. "There was no way to explain this to little third-graders in Riceville, Iowa. I knew I had to deal with this in a concrete way, not just talk about it, because we had talked about racism since the first day of school."

What happened in the classroom was shocking. Within fifteen minutes, the children who were "on top" became cruel and discriminatory against the "ones on bottom." Within twenty-four hours, there was a change in academic performance, based on whether students were the "smart ones" or the "dumb ones."

Reflecting on what they learned, the children in the class said things like: "I'll never be mean to someone because of their skin color." And: "It doesn't matter what someone's skin color is. You can't judge them on that." Experiencing discrimination made them anti-discriminatory. Reflecting on the experience as adults decades later, the lessons still resonated.

· · ·

Jeff and I greatly admired the work of Civil Rights activists. We wanted our children to understand what it felt like to be treated as outsiders in your own country. We were drawn to Jane Elliott's work, and we decided our students should experience this experiment, too. It would offer them a true understanding of discrimination in a personal and visceral way. As Jane Elliott said, "Reading or talking about it doesn't teach what it really means."

We knew we were taking a risk. Like the declaration of independence experience, this would be emotional. Little did we know just how emotional it would become for the Acton community and how much we would learn.

. . .

The week before we launched into Jane Elliott's "Blue Eyes/ Brown Eyes," we alerted the parents. We sent an email to them describing the exercise, along with the video of the PBS *Frontline* episode. We asked them not to talk about it first with their children so the experience could be as real and raw as possible. One of the newer parents emailed me right back: "Thank you for doing this! I'm excited for my daughter to experience it. I'm sure it will be hard but what a great lesson."

Kaylie and Anna had found their stride as Acton guides— creating projects and facilitating Socratically with ease. But this experience had them—and me—feeling more nervous than about anything we had yet done together. This would go against everything we held high: kindness, justice, and respect for each Eagle. We knew the key to success would be in the processing of the experiment after it happened, so we carved out special time for discussions as a group and for one-on-one discussions if needed.

When the students got settled the morning of the experiment, Kaylie dove right in: "We discovered a new report last night that proves children with brown eyes cannot become heroes. They are not smart or brave. Only children with blue eyes can become heroes."

The students' eyes got wide, and they quickly began looking around the circle to take note of eye color for the first time.

"Because our mission here at Acton is to equip young people to be heroes," she explained, "we can only spend our resources on those who will be successful."

For the rest of the day, blue-eyed Eagles would get extra snacks from the refrigerator. They needed to keep up their energy. They also would have special ice-water bottles in the fridge. Heroes need lots of exercise, she explained, so the blue-eyed Eagles get to have ten more minutes of free time and would get first choice of the balls and games.

"Brown-eyed Eagles cannot use the laptops today," she said. "They will need to do math only with worksheets and pencils. We need to save battery power for the students who will become heroes. Also, Brown-Eyes may not have any of the special snacks or ice water. I have these orange bands that we will tie around the arms of the Brown-Eyes so we can know who they are."

The classroom became very quiet. The usual buzz of energy was absent. Ms. Kaylie then said, "Okay. Let's get to work. It's core skills time and you know what to do."

What unfolded was painful to watch. At first, the "ones on top" had some fun with their privileged status. The snacks were yummy, and the Blue-Eyes made the most of their free time. But upon returning to the classroom, two of their friends were crying. Normally, the group rallied to help one another out. This time, they walked by and curled up with their books on the beanbags that were reserved for them. As the clocked ticked, rumblings of anger came through the tears. Charlie was one of the Brown-Eyes.

"I can think of a lot of heroes with brown eyes!" he said quite loudly. "This is not right! Jesus had brown eyes, I think!" Blossoming as a leader since his first day at Acton, Charlie continued: "Someone get a laptop and research the eye colors of heroes!" With his brown eyes, he was not able to use the laptop himself. Soon the group gathered around, yelling out the names of heroes and the colors of their eyes.

The guides and I were baffled. The Eagles had challenged the authority of the report! But we had a plan. Rather than switch the group that would be on top the next day, we decided to cut the experiment short. Kaylie called the group together.

"You are right," she said. "We got it wrong. The report actually said it was the brown-eyed people who were the smartest and most courageous. So we will switch the orange bands. Now the blue-eyed Eagles must wear them and go to their desks. No afternoon snacks or free time for the Blue-Eyes."

This time, there was a sense of fun. The children realized it was a game. But that feeling didn't last once the chocolate-chip cookies came out of the oven and only the "ones on top" got them. And then free time triggered the deep sense of injustice. The group heading outside began taunting the others: "Ha, ha! You are Blue-Eyes!"

The tears and anger began again. This time, though, both groups were feeling guilty about their behavior. They were distracted, not working, getting into arguments. The emotions were real and definitely raw. It was time to call it off and start processing what they had experienced.

"I hated when they laughed at me for having brown eyes. That was the worst part," Charlie said. "It wasn't fair and it made me so angry."

The group talked about what it meant to walk in someone else's shoes. How must people who are different feel when people are mean to them or make fun of them just because of their skin color?

"It must feel worse than what we were feeling," Sam said. "We only had to do this for a day. It must feel like you want to run away and hide. Maybe even die."

I was listening from the other room. This day meant more to me than any so far at Acton Academy. Sam Sandefer had found a voice. In his old school, he never said a word in a group discussion. One of my fears was that he would never find his own voice. He was a sensitive soul, shy, with tendencies toward anxiety. In addition, I feared he lived in the shadow of his older brother. But this day of emotional turmoil opened him up to share his voice. His words were strong and powerful. The group listened. Something was working. Sam was growing into himself and sharing his important thoughts with the world.

The guides led the processing of this experience with a level of compassion and mastery that was perfect. They let the students lead the way but coaxed honesty and openness from them. I was grateful that my children were there, having this unique and powerful experience that would last a lifetime. I thought the other parents would feel the same way.

I was very wrong. At the end of the day, seeing that her son was emotionally exhausted, one mother blurted out, "Isn't this abusive?"

My mind went back to Jane Elliott's original work back in the late 1960s. About 20 percent of the public reaction was visceral. One letter to her said, "How dare you try this cruel experiment out on white children! Black children grow up accustomed to such behavior, but white children, there's no way they could possibly understand it. It's cruel to white children and will cause them great psychological damage." Elliott developed her classroom exercise with the purpose of snuffing out this kind of racist talk.

What do we do with a parent who disagrees with the basis of experiential learning?

"We ask them to leave because we are unable to serve them anymore," Jeff said to me in an easy, straightforward way.

This was so far out of my comfort zone, but I could see that this parent was not a fit for our school. She would not be the first. We said good-bye. It hurt. I quickly learned I needed to be clearer in our application interviews that the Acton learning journey would be uncomfortable at times, even painful, as we watch the children struggle to learn. I would learn later how personal some parents' rejection of this kind of learning could be. This wasn't all kicks and giggles in our adorable schoolhouse.

I needed some good news.

Assessing ourselves: our weekly survey of Acton families

We have made transparency one of our key school values, and the Acton Academy families are well practiced in giving us regular and honest feedback. One of the most controversial practices at

Acton Academy, at least from the eyes of some traditional educators, is treating our families as valuable customers, whom we are delighted to serve. (The word "customer" riles up some people in very interesting ways, I have found.) While our relationship at Acton is, of course, far deeper than a transactional one, we never forget these parents are paying us to deliver on our promises. We need and want to know how they think we are doing in our service to them, so that we can continually improve.

To that end, each weekend, we send out an anonymous survey for our parents and students to rate us on their week at Acton. We ask them to give us comments on how we can improve. I open the results every Monday morning. I then send them out to the families so everyone gets to see how everyone else thinks we are doing as school owners.

These surveys help us to remain in a continual state of learning and improvement, just like each student and parent. We've been able to take what our parents and Eagles suggest and implement it when it fits into our mission.

My favorite requests were to add in more time for core skills work (children asking for more work time!) and a parent's request to be allowed to observe Socratic discussions so they could learn how to have them at home (children teaching adults!). Because of our commitment to student-driven learning, we can turn on a dime and change when they come up with something better that we believe is worth trying.

Bottom line: does Acton work?

For the children? According to standardized test scores, online dashboards, writing samples, and public demonstrations of work—yes. The Eagles have soared in their learning and are able to prove it to the world. We would soon discover one of the best ways to gauge learning: the apprenticeships the Eagles would experience when we opened our middle school and high school. To have small business owners and nonprofit leaders call us and request we send more Acton Eagles over to work with them has been one of our surest signs that our students are learning—and the community recognizes it.

For the parents? According to our families' survey results—yes, again. We've given more than 250 surveys with the question, "How satisfied were you with your experience at Acton Academy this week? Rate us 1–5 (with 1 being not satisfied, and 5 being extremely satisfied)." We've received an average score of 4.85 since our founding. Though we do receive a stinging comment now and then on our surveys, the overall rating tells me our families are generally happy and want to continue on with Acton, even though there are seasons of struggle in every student's learning process. I have learned that the Acton journey is not for everyone, and some parents opt out when the journey gets emotionally trying. But for those who stay and participate as optimistic partners with us, satisfaction is close to guaranteed.

Another telling evaluation was our Net Promoter Score to measure whether our Acton parents would recommend Acton Academy to a family or friend. This score is a standard measurement of loyalty for a brand. Apple, for example, had a very high Net Promoter Score of 76 percent in 2015. Costco's score that year was 78 percent. Acton Academy's most recent score was 100 percent—a rare level of satisfaction, to be sure.

Out of one abyss and into another

By the beginning of our third year, we had outgrown our sweet house and moved to temporary buildings on the campus of the Acton School of Business along the south shores of Lady Bird Lake. We had a three-year waiting list, and our oldest Eagles were aging out of elementary school.

It was time to open a middle school.

Chapter 7

MIDDLE SCHOOL
MONSTERS?

"If you were willing to allow me to open my own Acton, I would
do it not only for my own kids, but because I want all children to
have this opportunity. Once you experience your children loving to learn,
becoming independent, and happy, you can never not be a part of that."

—DANI FOLTZ-SMITH, ACTON ACADEMY PARENT AND OWNER OF
ACTON ACADEMY VENICE BEACH

On a Friday afternoon in late August 2012, I wrestled with a situation that threatened to scuttle the launch of our middle school, just a week away. We had fired our recently hired guide. He was unable to shake his traditional teacher tendencies, which included creating required reading lists and situating a large desk for himself in front of the room; our other guides didn't even have desks. We worked with him for months leading up to our launch; but the Socratic method of not answering questions was proving to be too big a struggle for him. He thought he should tell students the right answers rather than waiting for the students to figure them out. The last straw was when he told us a disturbing story about how he handled a disagreement with a middle school student by using intimidation—an attitude that went against everything we believed in, no matter how rough he said the school environment and this child were.

We understood; giving children the opportunity to make their own decisions and claim the consequences was not natural for most adults. But without him, we were left in a lurch.

Jeff and I racked our brains for a replacement, the pressure building with every passing hour.

"I've had an epiphany," I said.

"What?"

"You."

"Me what?"

"You are going to be the lead guide for the middle school," I said. "What a coup for our parents and Eagles to have you as their guide. You are one of the best in the country!"

Jeff was a dedicated student of the Socratic method, and he had been weaning himself away from his teaching load at the Acton School of Business for a while so that other entrepreneurs could take the reins there.

"This could be your next calling," I said. "A middle school guide."

Silence. He percolated.

"I'll do it," he said in what came off as a confident tone.

Jeff spent that night regretting his response. Sure, he knew how to lead a class of elite MBA students in a Socratic discussion about entrepreneurship; but how would that translate to middle school students with reading, writing, math, and science? And didn't most traditional teachers steer clear of middle school, knowing that it was an awkward time for everyone? In education circles, as one principal told me, middle school kids were known as "monsters" for a reason.

And if he failed it would be especially painful, because his own sons would be in the studio.

The next morning, Jeff said he was at peace: "I'm all in."

. . .

Teenagers were a completely new population for us, and I had many questions about how self-governance would work with young people who are socially self-conscious, more interested in covering each other's backs than holding each other accountable to excellence. The gripping narrative of the Hero's Journey worked so well with young children and older adults; but I had no idea how maturing teenagers would take to it. Would it seem trite?

Not only that, the middle school "studio," our term for *class-room*, had to look and feel different from our elementary school studio. It had to feel "older." Yet the design had to imbue the same purpose: self-governed young people bound by contracts and working toward specific goals.

On a more trivial note, I had to beat the competition's rite of passage for middle school—the exciting shift to getting a locker. It seemed this was a sign of new independence. All the public middle schools had lockers, and the young teenagers in town were chatty and excited about decorating their lockers. We, however, would not have lockers. Acton Academy's middle school would look more like a tech start-up's office space, with long tables and rolling chairs. If only I had known that rolling chairs could become bumper cars. Bad design idea on my part.

. . .

On the first day, our fresh band of fourteen middle school Eagles walked one by one down a long entry path flanked with photos of their greatest heroes. Jack, Pace, Charlie, Jasper, Crayton, Coby, James, Kenzie, Hayes, Ellie, Sarah, Ana, Claire, and Mason were our founding middle school Eagles.

Their studio stood next door to the elementary studio, where the younger children were playing freely and already enjoying themselves. The older students looked timid and hopeful, stopping to examine each photo as if trying to delay entering the studio for one minute more.

During the summer, we had asked every new middle school Eagle to send Jeff the name of their personal hero and a quote about why they admired that person. We purchased white cardboard signs and created a Hero Board for each new Eagle. Their names were printed boldly at the top, and large photographs of their heroes were flanked by the Eagles' personal quotes. The boards were secured to posts and planted in the ground to line the path from the parking lot to their new studio door.

The Hero Boards would become a tradition for celebrating the gifts and dreams of each new Eagle, providing identity and a place for those unsure about their new community. They also served as a source of curiosity and questions to begin bonding each new Eagle to the tribe.

We started the first morning just like we had in the elementary school—with a Socratic launch, our term for a discussion on a theme for the day that sets the tone for learning. This happened at precisely 8:30 a.m.

"Why are we all here?" Jeff asked. "What matters most to you—having more freedom, discovering a special gift, or changing the world in a profound way?"

The next leg of our journey had begun.

. . .

For the first few weeks, the middle school Eagles concentrated on the fundamentals—reading, writing, math—and building the tribe. Jeff organized team-building exercises, including an off-site ropes course, and pulled activities from the Acton MBA curriculum designed to get them started on learning more about themselves.

Many educators assume teenagers go to school to learn or prepare for life. We learned quickly that most young people just want to be with their friends. So our goal was to make it fun to be part of the Acton tribe and to make the first few weeks feel like the start of an adventure. Once Eagles wanted to belong to the tribe and were eager to start a journey together, the guides could make hard work a requirement for staying. The simple ethos was, work hard to earn your freedom and have a lot of fun along the way.

Their daily schedule was similar in design to that of the elementary school. Mornings were for quiet core skills work. Afternoons were for collaborative, hands-on projects. In between were Socratic discussions for history, writing workshops, and free time.

"How can you teach history through Socratic discussions

led by children?" asked a guest observing one day from a local high school.

Jeff replied, "In fact, it's the student-led discussions that are the secret sauce to learning history. The key is the moral dilemma. We put a young person in the shoes of a historical hero facing a difficult decision with an important moral issue at stake. Even better, that same moral issue is vexing leaders today and (separately) matters to the young person in his or her own life."

The guest seemed eager to hear more, so Jeff went on. "The bottom line is this: We're not teaching history. We're giving young people the tools to make better moral decisions; and to do so, they need to dig deeply into what happened in the past. The motivation makes all the difference, as does the goal of 'learning to do' something—make better moral decisions—instead of 'learning dead history.' When we get the questions right, young people will spend hours on the research—and with a little preparation, they'll hold a self-organized, high-energy debate about what matters in life."

Early on, the middle school Eagles surprised us. While it wasn't Utopia, this group often worked and played together like highly functioning adults.

"It's dawned on me that middle schoolers aren't monsters at all," Jeff said. "They can be responsible, creative people—as fun to be around as a roomful of ambitious Harvard or Acton MBAs."

However, there were soon signs of trouble.

Testing boundaries

We know standardized tests have little correlation with lifelong achievement, but they provide benchmarks for improvement. By administering a test at the beginning and end of each year, we have a measure of improvement that quantifies the real growth of our students, growth that we see every day, including in their projects and exhibitions.

This sort of test would be a departure from Acton's routine and our typical approach to learning. So it was not surprising that the first time we tested the middle school students, they immediately reverted to the expectations of an adult-centered, teacher-driven system. We didn't see this reaction in the younger group of Eagles who just took the test in stride, almost like a funny activity. There was no preparation or teaching to the test. We simply emailed their parents the night before and told them what we planned on doing. But the older Eagles suddenly acted like students with a teacher in a classroom; they started asking lots of questions and seemed helpless until a teacher gave them answers.

"Where can I find a pencil?"

"Is it okay to erase a wrong answer?"

"Can I use a scratch pad?"

The test instructions were crystal-clear. Moments before, these young heroes had powered through self-paced math problems, led Socratic discussions, organized janitorial duties, and drafted self-governing documents; yet they became infantilized by the testing process, asking for the most minute directions.

The free time after the test saw an explosion of pent-up

energy, as chaos overtook the studio. The students' behavior began to spiral out of control.

One of the middle schoolers approached Jeff. "Would you please do something?"

"It's your studio, not mine," Jeff told him. "What are you going to do about it?"

The student wavered, so Jeff rephrased the question, offering a choice: "Should you act alone or see if there are some other leaders who want to join you?"

The Eagle got the message and quickly called an emergency meeting of the studio leaders. Everyone showed up. He reiterated the verbal promises each had made and appealed to the most disruptive Eagles to keep their word. Order was restored—at least for the time being.

"First, you make it fun to belong. Then you let the tribe set its standards," Jeff told the other guides later. "You have to hold up a mirror when the group or some individuals fail to keep a promise."

Jeff found that the key was to keep experimenting with different combinations of incentives and boundaries, individually and for the group, each announced in advance; his intent was to keep from triggering that sense of adolescent injustice that arose quickly when the students found themselves being ordered about by adults—especially without good reason.

"If they are in charge and making choices, they are motivated to challenge themselves and one another," Jeff told me. "They can learn at warp speed. But if they see adults taking control and running things, they get back in the mode of doing nothing. It's a delicate balance."

The first round of test results was surprising. Approximately half the class was in the bottom 10 percent of test scores—shockingly low in reading and writing ability. The other half hovered near the top 1 percent. It seemed we had attracted either those bored by conventional school or those failing dismally—with few, if any, in between.

. . .

Before long, middle school had a rhythm of simple core skills practices. They were keeping track of math skills earned on Khan Academy, daily pages read in a favorite book, writing challenges shared in peer critiques, and Socratic discussions about important turning points in civilization.

The first middle schoolers' hands-on project was focused on building a mini-civilization—their own—during the first few weeks of the year. They developed guidelines for the studio, including rules of engagement for studio discussions, such as "Listen," "Be concise," and "Provide evidence." They created a process for cleaning and organizing the studio and put "champions" in charge of checking up on the work to ensure their space was left in pristine order each day. They got to know each other and listened to daily stories about the Hero's Journey. As in the elementary studio, we integrated PE and creative arts to round out their work and create opportunities for personal growth.

At the end of five weeks together, they were ready to write their studio Contract. They had the elementary school's document as a standard, and it was a high one. This document would be the studio authority. It would define the boundaries of behavior, character traits, and attitude.

As a Socratic guide, Jeff held to the strict code of conduct—promising to never answer a question, no matter how practical or necessary. Keeping this promise was hard, especially when the studio became disorderly, which was happening with the older students more often than the younger ones. The pull of entropy is strong, and the middle school Eagles' intentionality to work hard kept fraying. Cleanup time in the afternoons resulted in a less and less pristine studio. Collaboration during core skills time routinely deteriorated into wasting time with friends.

Jeff felt like his hands were tied. He decided to ask for a small group of middle school Eagles to volunteer for an observation mission into the elementary school to try to understand why their culture kept falling into chaos while the elementary school's held together. Why was it harder for them to establish the same work habits that the elementary students exhibited?

They would return to the studio with ideas, and each new attempt injected energy for a day or two, but the commitment would soon decay. *Lord of the Flies* moments cropped up weekly.

Mall cop

Charlie was not afraid to question authority, nor did he shy away from challenging his fellow students when he thought they were coming up short. He enlisted himself on a mission to keep the middle school's standards high.

"That costs an Eagle Buck for each of you," he said to two

Eagles who were having a side conversation during a Socratic discussion. Jeff had injected "Eagle Bucks" into studio life as an incentive for the students to work hard and to hold each other accountable. They could earn Bucks for accomplishing work goals and then spend their earnings on treats like snacks or buying more free time. An Eagle could lose Bucks for breaking the rules. But the Eagles themselves had to be the ones to deliver the fines, not the guide. There was a bank and a committee of students to manage the distribution and collection of Eagle Bucks; this took the delivery of "discipline" out of the hands of an adult and gave the young people a way to manage each other—if everyone participated in the system.

Later that day, as Charlie walked past a cluster of desks, he saw an Eagle playing videogames instead of working. "That's an Eagle Buck," he said, as the offender slammed his laptop closed.

"Quit being a mall cop," one of the Eagles said to him. Charlie had not yet learned that leadership is a balance between tough-mindedness and warm-heartedness. He had the tough-minded part down and had no problem calling his peers out on being distracting at every turn. To him, he was just calling things as he saw them. But it didn't sit well with the other Eagles. The "mall cop" label stuck.

Jeff coached him along, asking him to let others be the voice of accountability and generally helping with what "warm-hearted" leadership looked like.

It would be three more years before we'd see how Charlie's growth from mall cop to true leader would play out.

Elementary intervention

The middle school tribe was setting its own standards. But these standards were neither good enough nor being held strongly enough for some of the original and younger Eagles. A rebellion was brewing in the elementary school, led by our son Sam, who had found a strong and steady voice and cared deeply about the standards of excellence at Acton Academy. So did Bodhi, Chris, and Saskia, who were also in the elementary school; they had seen Charlie, Ellie, and Cash move on to middle school.

"The middle schoolers are ruining Acton," he said a few weeks into the new session. "They don't work hard, they distract us all the time, and they don't follow the Contract."

Sam informed us at the kitchen table that the elementary school Eagles had written a letter and signed a petition asking the middle school Eagles to leave.

"We've elected an ambassador and a commission to deliver the petition," he said. "Can we do that tomorrow?"

Sam was speaking with a seriousness I'd never seen in him. He was protective of Acton Academy and its culture of learning and excellence. He was becoming a thoughtful and persuasive leader with a quiet but strong voice.

Charlie shot back: "Sam, I can handle it."

"Well, why haven't you then?" asked Sam.

The next day, a group of elementary Eagles approached the middle school with the petition. They had collected evidence over a period of weeks to prove the middle school standards were too low for Acton Academy. They were detracting from the Acton name, which the younger Eagles held in such esteem. The older Eagles' studio was a mess compared with the younger

Eagles' studio. There were library books all over the floor. The microwave had old food stuck inside that emitted an unpleasant odor. The supply cart was a complete mess—pens and pencils broken and stuffed under the copy paper tray. Much worse than the appearance of the studio was the level of noise during work time. The walls between the studios were thin, and the younger Eagles were having a hard time focusing on their work because of the bad work habits of the older Eagles.

This was a rude awakening for the middle school tribe.

Jeff led a discussion with the group. "Well, you've all read the elementary studio petition, alleging you've damaged their property rights by being a poor neighbor. In the real world, you could be facing Chapter 7 or Chapter 11 bankruptcy," he explained.

Fourteen pairs of eyes went wide. Whatever bankruptcy was, it didn't sound good. "Why don't you take thirty minutes and research what bankruptcy might mean for the middle school?"

The group reconvened a half hour later, and Jeff asked, "So what's the difference between Chapter 7 or Chapter 11 bankruptcy?"

Ellie said, "Chapter 7 bankruptcy is about liquidation, which I think means the middle school would disappear and Chapter 11 means reorganization. I think that means starting over."

"In this instance, we'd declare Chapter 11 bankruptcy, because there's something worth saving," Jeff said. Everyone in the room relaxed, until he added, "Which means three elementary Eagles will be appointed as your overseers, to make sure the studio runs smoothly as we reorganize."

Problem solved. The thought of being led by seven- and

eight-year-olds was enough to jolt the middle school leaders back to a high level of personal responsibility for running their studio.

The elementary school Eagles were right on target and their insurrection proved to be a turning point. I was learning again that sometimes it is the youngest who speak the truth and create change.

Bucking the trend

"Witnessing the chaos is so difficult for me," Jeff told me one night after a particularly trying day. "It's just disheartening when the studio turns messy and mean. Some days I just want to give up."

It was time to add more clarity and structure, some risks and rewards. Jeff designed and introduced a crude economic system based on poker chips. "I am always setting up games and inviting students to play," he said. "If they don't work, I design a new one."

Jeff organized the Eagles into three-person squads. Each Eagle received three chips per week. Each infraction of studio rules that governed "listening" and "respect" triggered the loss of a chip. If everyone wasn't in place for the opening discussion at 8:30 a.m. or the studio wasn't pristine by the 3:00 p.m. closing, everyone lost a chip. If every member of a squad had a chip on Friday, the entire squad received a treat. Squad members could loan one another chips, but only if there were consequences in place for the loan.

The poker chip game translated into equipping the Eagles to

better understand and use the power of Eagle Bucks. They had never practiced how to use them, and like with any new system there was a learning curve. There were days when Eagle Bucks caused personal conflicts between students and there were days when they worked like a charm to keep the group working hard and holding boundaries. As time went on, they decided the system, even if flawed, was much better than needing to revert to having adults order them around.

Sam came home one day and decided it would be a good idea for the elementary studio to have Eagle Bucks, too. "Good idea, Sam! Why don't you figure out how to implement that and introduce it to your group at the next Town Hall Meeting?" I said, happy to see him rising to the occasion to help the younger Eagles become even more student-driven.

Town Hall Meetings became part of the Acton weekly structure during our first year. In those early days, Kaylie or Anna would lead and manage the discussion of issues in the studio—from people distracting each other to how they could celebrate the end of a session. By the fourth year, the Eagles had taken over the facilitation of these weekly meetings. Organized, disciplined, and important discussions are led by an Eagle, who chairs the meeting. The agenda is created by Eagles earlier in the week through a system of completing a form, specifying either an announcement to be read out loud at the meeting or a problem that needs to be discussed and resolved in the meeting. The forms are collected in a box, and before the meeting begins, the chairperson of the meeting collects them and sets the agenda.

In my years of leading Acton, these weekly Town Hall Meetings have proven over and over that children can do far more than we ever imagine or allow. They can decide what's fair in distributing scarce resources, such as dodge balls or green space. They can assess and weigh options for how to fix a flaw in layout of the studio. They can disagree with each other respectfully, and they can delegate responsibility based on skills and experience. They run efficient and effective meetings. And they function much better when the adults stay quiet and turn over this leadership in an authentic way.

"Learning design"—chaos into order

Despite the cultural challenges, the middle school Eagles were learning as much and as rapidly as the younger Eagles. Just as in the elementary school, students were encouraged to read anything they found fun. We set aside time specifically dedicated to reading and to discussing which books they'd recommend to a friend. Soon every Eagle was reading—a lot. The first year, the average middle schooler devoured sixteen books; even the least-engaged reader finished seven. At one point, *Democracy in America, 1984, Animal Farm, Madame Bovary, The Catcher in the Rye, The Screwtape Letters,* and *Anna Karenina* were scattered around the studio.

The middle school Eagles practiced journaling and creative writing, with frequent sharing and feedback. At this point, there were only rudimentary online grammar programs and very little game-based writing software available, so we used small group workshops for editing support. We quickly learned that the more the Eagles shared, the more they wanted to write, and the more they wanted to write, the more interested they were in using various tools to improve.

Jeff introduced a classic writer's-workshop process that has a predictable flow:

- Idea generation
- Rough draft
- Critique
- Revision
- Critique
- Editing
- Publication

The Eagles critiqued one another on ideas, organization, word choice, sentence fluency, voice, and conventions (grammar) and ranked the use of traits from strongest to weakest.

Math was straightforward, too. We used Khan Academy to deliver math skills with no guide interaction and to allow each Eagle to move at his or her own pace. For example, one of our middle school Eagles pushed through pre-algebra in only three weeks, while another struggled with an early traditional school math deficit but soon found a new stride and began to love math, moving five grade levels in ten months. "I was told I was bad at math," she said to me one day. "I'm not! I just have to work hard at it."

The traditional academic path to study science is criticized by some because it often presents it as a subject area to be memorized, making it seem more like answers to life's important questions rather than a form of logical inquiry.

In the middle school studio, we introduced science through Thomas Kuhn's paradigm shifts, where the frameworks that make sense today are expected to be overthrown tomorrow.

Eagles could then separate scientists into three archetypes: *paradigm busters*, revolutionaries like Galileo and Einstein, who bravely turned an established view of science upside down; *puzzle makers*, who proposed theories to shore up or disprove a paradigm; and *data collectors*, the careful and meticulous scientists who carefully gathered and recorded data, making the other groups' work possible.

We then could debate whether discovery (paradigm busting); invention (puzzle making); collecting data (data collectors), or innovation—non-scientist entrepreneurs bringing science into the real world by spreading inventions—add the most value to the world.

We began to introduce more difficult real-world challenges, requiring more difficult skills like probability analysis and film-making. By design, the problems were messier and required more teamwork. While the stakes were high to deliver top-notch exhibitions because parents and visitors were in the audience, even more important were the self-management and self-governance lessons that began to emerge as the Eagles realized the necessity of converting chaos into order.

We had no idea this would be one of the more powerful outcomes of what was beginning to be called "the Acton way"— chaos into order and back again. A cycle that the Eagles were beginning to predict, resolve, and manage on their own rather than depending on adults to mandate it from the top down. Understanding this freed us to embrace the times of chaos, knowing that learning was happening because the students were connected and engaged with their emotions, even if those emotions included stress and frustration.

The most impactful learning experience also became the greatest incentive and culture enhancer for the middle school group: apprenticeships. Knowing the last quarter of the year would be spent finding real jobs suddenly made spelling, proper English, persuasive word choice, and responsible time management seem very important to this young group. They were writing letters and accomplishing goals not just for a grade; they were working to get hired. By early May, Eagles each had an apprenticeship secured in a wide variety of places, including a ranch, a bakery, a veterinary clinic, a graphic design shop, an architectural firm, a preschool, and a news station. Want an engaged, serious teenager? Let them do real work they care about.

The results are in

The first line of Jeff's email to me read: "Here are the test scores."

I guess you could call this a moment of truth. After the pretest from the beginning of the first year showed the middle school Eagles divided into the highest and lowest percentiles of achievement, I dreaded seeing this next round of scores. What if the initially underperforming student hadn't improved? Worse, what if the high-level students had joined the others at the bottom? I scanned the report. On average, Acton Academy students tested three grade levels above age before maxing out the test. *This is crazy,* I thought to myself. *It really works.*

The gains were dramatic and would continue over time. Lower-performing students typically advanced two or three grade levels in math and reading each year, until middle schoolers reached post–high school level.

Of course, we had far too little data to stand up to any serious academic study. But Jeff and I and the other Acton parents didn't care—we could see the transformation that was happening in our children right before our eyes.

We ended our first year of middle school developing the capstone piece of the Acton Academy learning journey—a series of badges that represented long-term bodies of work by the Eagles in reading, writing, math, projects and quests (sciences, arts, technology, entrepreneurship, finance, and engineering), civilization (history, economics, government), and servant leadership (mentoring, coaching and guiding other Eagles). The badges were designed to be modular, like Legos. The type and amount of work necessary to earn a badge could be clearly defined, while leaving many choices up to the Eagles. This preserved both freedom of choice and excellence. Eagles could prove their skills to the world and be able to choose the challenges they found compelling.

The development of the badges would be critical for our creation of a high school. Each one included requirements from a traditional course and could be translated into a transcript that other schools, colleges, and universities could interpret easily.

Each child at Acton, including the youngest six-year-olds, would have a Badge Plan that parents could see, understand, and track. Another layer of complexity, yes, but one that raised the standards of everything we were doing. The detailed descriptions of requirements to earn a badge made visible to the world the rich, deep, and rigorous learning an Acton Eagle would achieve (see appendix G).

The successful addition of an Acton middle school was a big step forward. We could forge ahead building and improving it, knowing that soon we'd be doing the same for a high school. Just as I began seeing the light at the end of the tunnel for building up our "dream school," a darkness that would change everything was creeping into my personal life—a life that had become inextricably bound to everything Acton Academy.

CHAPTER 8

LOST *in the* DARKNESS

"Our daughter was showing signs of depression before attending Acton Academy. She is now happy and thriving, in large part because of the Acton way of learning. Now, she loves school so much that she never wants to miss a day."

—SUSANNAH HOLLINGER, ACTON ACADEMY PARENT

Sam and Charlie were mistaken for twins the first six years of their lives. While their physical appearances blended together, their personalities stood starkly apart.

"I'm done."

With that, two-and-a-half-year-old Charlie stood up from the crowd of toddlers at the library story time and began walking out of the room. He'd simply had enough of the exaggerated voice and methodical reading of the librarian. There were more exciting things to do with his time, and he knew it.

Charlie has a truly independent, decision-making spirit. He'd said out loud what I had been thinking at the same moment. I was done, too, but would have sat there, politely, thinking it was the right thing to do. Not Charlie. He has been driven and vocal since day one.

He also carries his father's peculiar bent toward not caring what people think about him. He's kind and extremely thoughtful but has no qualms about clearly stating his ideas. He has absolute confidence in walking alone.

Sam's typical response was more cautious. He said, "No, thank you," when I signed him up for three-year-old soccer. All of his friends were going to be on the team, and so I went through the motions as all moms did. You simply signed your kid up for soccer, right? Not Sam, though. It wasn't until he watched from the sidelines for a year that he decided soccer was something he wanted to try.

Sam is an observer of life. He watches, listens, gathers information, and then—only then—does he make a decision. But once the decision is made, he doesn't waver. This plays out interestingly in a family of daredevils.

Paragliding, for example, is one of our favorite summer activities. We trek with tandem pilots to the top of a mountain, strap in, and run until the wind picks us up to soar into the clouds. Charlie started tandem flying at age three after watching me do it once. So, we thought that Sam, too, would love to fly when he turned three.

That year, he rode up the mountain with us. Dave, Sam's wildly charming, uber-talented paragliding pilot, chatted with him on the drive all the way up the mountain about what he needed to do when we got to the top. He talked to a three-year-old with exactly the right dose of respect and humor. They unpacked the paraglider, and Dave got them all strapped in and ready for takeoff. Suddenly, Sam looked back at him with his dark serious eyes. "No, thank you," he said.

Dave unstrapped them, packed up the gear, and drove Sam down the mountain for an ice cream cone. It took Sam three more years of watching us before he said, "Yes, please." We learned as time went on that Sam's deliberate decision making contributed to a deep sense of commitment once a decision was made.

The winter of discontent

Acton Academy's sixth year included our progression toward a grand opening of Launchpad—Acton Academy's high school, named by the rising middle school Eagles. It was also a year filled with frustration for Charlie Sandefer.

As he approached the end of middle school, our older son's demeanor changed. He became quiet, tired, slow to laugh. His regular funny rants to morning talk radio on the way to school stopped. He didn't say anything at all. I feared his fire had gone out—the one thing I was trying to protect by building this school.

The culture of the middle school Eagles was strikingly different from that of the elementary school he helped create, and Charlie began to have trouble reconciling his own place there. He was feeling disconnected from the tribe. For the first time since 2009, he sensed a negative aura in the Acton studio. There was a sub-tribe forming of Eagles who didn't want to work at all. And Charlie was caught in the middle.

"I don't want to talk about school anymore," he told us at the dinner table.

Charlie had grown into a straightforward, hardworking

young man. Tall, lean, and focused, he took after both parents in his dedication to a mission and "get it done" attitude. Under Jeff's coaching, he had risen above being a mall cop and had cultivated a quiet leadership that encouraged others to shine. But he cringed at how a small group of his peers shunned work and skirted through loopholes in the Contract.

After dinner, we'd sit on the couch, and Charlie would often share frustrations about his experience. He had been defending the studio contract since he helped write it with the other founding students back in 2009. He was getting tired of feeling alone in making the older group of Eagles work better together.

Rather than complain anymore, he hunkered down and worked harder. But I could tell he was headed toward a breaking point.

At the same time, Sam had experienced a physical illness and hospitalization that had spiraled into a deep state of anxiety. My darkest moments as a parent were watching him suffer without understanding why and not knowing how to support him or ease his pain. I began wondering if the Acton way of learning was simply too hard. Did we cause his suffering? Were we expecting too much?

And then there was Taite, who had chosen to live full-time with her mom, leaving us with a sense of emptiness that no level of thinking or planning would ever fill.

Layered on top of the hurts at home was the realization that starting a school sets one up to be a target of blame when things don't go well for a family. I had received emails laced with vindictive language and been cut from social circles. "Why didn't we open an ice cream store and just make people happy all day?" I asked Jeff one day. "This work weighs heavily on me."

"I'm done"

At 5:30 one dark winter morning, I was sitting in my bedroom reading when Charlie walked in.

"Mom," he said, "I want to go somewhere else for high school."

All I could muster was, "Thank you so much for coming to me. Let's wait until tonight to talk with Dad about this."

I couldn't bear to break this news to Jeff. Our elder son—who had been one of the reasons we started this work in the first place—actually wanted to break away. My heart broke wide open.

But Charlie's decision was not a complete surprise. He had been sharing his frustrations about feeling disconnected from the group for some time. But how had it gotten so bad? What was he running away from? Had we completely failed?

Our sons, Charlie and Sam, were our pillars at Acton Academy. We started it for them, and they had become our canaries in the coal mine. Around the dinner table and on lazy weekends, we'd hash out how things were going in the studio. And when we introduced new programs or quests, Charlie and Sam provided the truth serum. Did our new ideas work in real time, or did they fall flat? We had depended on them every step of the way to inspire us and to share what was working and what was not. They had been our teachers and guides.

A shimmer of hope was that Sam was still "in." As the clouds of his anxiety lifted, so did his commitment to his learning journey at Acton. In fact, he had come out the other side of that dark tunnel with a grounded sense of purpose and a desire to lead others. Along with him, we had almost seventy other young people at Acton who were lights in my life each day. My dedication to my own children's learning had morphed into a dedication to all children's.

But the Acton journey ahead would not include dear Charlie. *This was not how I wanted our story to go.*

The end of the day came, and I knew I had to tell Jeff.

"Charlie told me this morning he doesn't want to go to Launchpad. He wants to look at other high schools in town."

"Well, he can do that, but I'm not paying for him to go to another private school." Jeff's response jolted me. We were so used to listening to the children and considering their input. The schools Charlie wanted to apply to were, indeed, the private ones, but that was not the point right now. This was more complex than a financial choice. No matter how much we say we trust the children in the learning environment, being a parent is hard; there is a balance to be found between being permissive and authoritarian. A parent can trust a child, but that doesn't mean he or she turns authority in the family over to the child. Parents are not Socratic guides. It's not healthy for family life to center on a child's wants all the time. Jeff and I never claimed to be perfect parents, and we struggle like all parents with knowing when to claim authority and when to let the children figure things out on their own. I sensed the direct clarity of Jeff's response was a cover for his own muddled feelings about Charlie's decision.

In this tender moment, we were both at a loss.

· · ·

When Charlie came to me that dark morning to announce his desire to leave Acton, I could see the resolve in his eyes. In a sense, Charlie had taken command of his education. The initial shock I felt at this announcement progressed into stages of grief—denial, anger, some bargaining with God, and, finally, a sweet acceptance and realization. What stood before me was not the six-year-old child who loved trucks more than anything. He was a young man who had become an independent learner and could make solid decisions. Here was someone who could claim his dreams and make plans to achieve them, a person who could understand what he needed to learn in order to be complete. Charlie had proven he could work extremely hard and was not afraid to begin a new adventure on his own.

Charlie's decision to leave Acton disrupted our lives in more ways than one. For more than a week, Jeff stuck to his initial reaction. He simply went quiet on the subject. We never discussed it, as if it never had been brought up.

Concerned that he had not heard me on that ill-fated evening, I said to him, "I think you need to listen wholeheartedly to Charlie. This is really important to him, and he's being brave to take a stand and to think about his own journey differently than we are. I am going to help him in this process. He's going to apply to two other private schools."

I walked away thinking that there was a solid chance I'd be fighting for Charlie alone. I thought I should be standing in solidarity with Jeff, but he had not seen Charlie's eyes on that morning. He had not heard the tone in his voice.

Greener grass?

Charlie and I had a month to hit the application deadlines for the two private high schools he was considering. There were entrance exams to take, essays to write, applications to complete, interviews and tours to attend.

My life as I'd lived it for the past eight years now suddenly seemed so simple and focused. I was entering the blur of traditional school bureaucracies and was reminded of how free I had felt as an Acton parent. All of a sudden I was hearing about detention policies and absence restrictions.

My reality was now divided. I woke up every day and greeted Eagles at the curb, coached guides, and witnessed learning happening. I was the Acton Academy head of school. I had that hat and wanted to wear it well. And soon we were launching a high school. How could I face other parents who wondered about applying to it? I couldn't imagine having to say, "Yes! Acton's fabulous! We built it for our son. Oh, but he chose not to go here. But believe me, it's great."

At the same time, I was rushing with Charlie to tour schools and attend admissions interviews. How could I sit with Charlie in those interviews and honestly say I agreed with their programming and that I supported his desire to go there? How could I answer the questions on the applications about why I was choosing that school and what I planned to contribute as a parent?

And finally, after a long day at Acton, I'd come home to Jeff. We weren't talking much about what was going on. Charlie kept pushing through the application procedures, and Jeff was quiet— except when he would remind me: "I'm not paying for this."

The school Charlie chose to attend was in many ways quite

the opposite of Acton Academy—a private school with a classical Christian curriculum, mandatory uniforms, chapel, frequent quizzes, tests, a focus on college preparation, and a high value placed on obedience to authority. Charlie was drawn to the vision of having real teachers and high school sports. He wanted to see if he could sit and learn in a classroom like everyone else seemed to do. Maybe most importantly, he didn't want to have to be the leader all the time and hold standards for other kids his age.

The question for me was clear: Could the fledgling culture of the Acton middle school and high school survive and grow without Charlie's daily presence and vocal persistence to keep the promises in the studio contract?

Jeff comes around

Charlie was sitting on the couch at home one day when Jeff came in and sat down next to him. It had been two weeks since Charlie announced his desire to leave Acton. During that time, Jeff had been on an internal odyssey of his own. While wrestling with how much freedom to give Charlie and waging his personal battle against the traditional education system, he realized he had been suppressing his son's inner spirit—the one thing he did not want to do.

"Charlie, I've made a decision," he said. "I'm going to fully support your choice to go to another school. I'll miss you dearly at Acton but will pay for you to attend elsewhere. I've thought a lot about this and you need to do this. I need to let you have your own journey."

As I listened in from the kitchen, all I could feel was *relief*. We were united again as a family, rather than living as a divided front. I wasn't happy we were losing Charlie at Acton, but at least we were supporting each other's individual life paths and embracing the strain together.

We kept the applications to other schools a secret from the Acton community as long as we could. It just didn't seem necessary for the world to know. It was still difficult to explain how the head of the school's own son could leave that school.

Charlie's decision to leave was particularly hard to take because we knew he would thrive in Launchpad, which would be more like working at a creative start-up company than attending a school. The studio would be mostly managed by the teenagers themselves, with lots of freedom and with leadership opportunities to guide and mentor the younger Eagles in both the middle school and elementary school studios.

Our designed structure of the Launchpad day was similar to that in the elementary and middle school studios but with more time spent in real-world apprenticeships. These ambitious teenagers would continue to hone core skills each morning through online programs, reading deep books, writing even more complex genre pieces, and tackling upper-level math subjects like probability and statistics and calculus. They would also engage in Socratic discussions to explore deeply important questions about what made civilizations rise and fall, and they'd continue studying American and world history. Their afternoons would be spent in collaborative work, participating in more advanced quests (a deeper form of "projects") in biology, chemistry, and physics, which included online college course components.

We also had joined a private school athletics association so our older Eagles could compete with other schools in flag football, basketball, and soccer. They would each earn First Aid and CPR certification and have the opportunity for an annual expedition—international or national—planned and executed by the group of Eagles and funded by money they earned during apprenticeships.

As the name implied, Launchpad was preparing these teenagers for their next adventure after graduation. They would receive personal coaching to help dig deeper into their dreams and life goals as well as spend more time in apprenticeships to gain real-world experience within industries of their particular interest. These young people would launch into the world equipped and prepared to fulfill their plans. Most were planning to attend a competitive college and would graduate with a substantial number of college credits.

But Charlie would not be experiencing this vision in action.

Exodus and support

The other Eagles could tell that something in Charlie had changed. They started asking him about whether he was staying for Launchpad. The day we got the acceptance letter from Charlie's new high school, we decided it was time to get ahead of the gossip. I wrote a blog post about Charlie's decision and waited for the comments and emails to roll in. It now felt more real. Charlie was leaving Acton.

The response came in slowly—supporting Charlie. One mom

in particular helped me gain some perspective: "My husband and I were talking about it, and we realized neither one of us would want to go to high school where our parents were the teachers and principal! We wish Charlie the best."

I made a slideshow for just the four of us—me, Jeff, and the boys—called "Acton Academy with Charlie." I had collected photos from every year and put them together to mark this milestone. On the eve of his last day, we watched it together. I tried to hold back tears. Jeff smiled. Charlie laughed and annotated the scenes.

Sam didn't say a word. He had never expressed much of an opinion about Charlie's decision. I wondered if he was relieved to be out from under Charlie's shadow. *Maybe this is the best thing for both of them*, I thought.

As the slideshow ended, we laughed over the memories of the declaration of independence rebellion. We moaned over memories of Eagle Buck mishaps and Charlie's "mall cop" label. We congratulated Charlie for surviving it all and contributing so much of himself to our mission.

The next day, at closing group in the middle school, Jeff asked Charlie and another departing Eagle who had been with us for years to stand in front of the group with him. Jeff wanted to mark their departure with words of gratitude for what they had given in their time at Acton. But it got deep and personal very quickly.

He started to read his personal statement but made it through only a few lines. He pounded his chest with his fist, because the words would not come out. Tears rolled down his cheeks.

"I'm sorry," he finally said. "I didn't expect to be so emotional.

We are grateful to both of you. We will miss you dearly. We wish you heroic journeys."

It was the first time I'd ever seen Jeff cry.

Charlie had served as both our test case and our truth teller. We needed the culture to be redefined without him. Though we felt fear about doing this without Charlie's leadership, our zeal did not waver. Sam was coming up through the middle school, and the thought of his future in this unpredictable and drastically changing world steadied our determination to get Launchpad right.

I asked Sam if he thought he'd want to look elsewhere for high school like Charlie did. His indomitable commitment to his personal decision making shone through.

"Charlie's crazy," he said. "I'm staying at Acton."

CHAPTER 9

MORE PARENTS PICK UP *the* TORCH

"The fact that Acton demands excellence and mastery is the ONLY reason our daughter could even dream of applying to a top university. At Acton, she was not handicapped by being a 'late bloomer.' She has had both the room to find herself and the accountability to rise up. Acton is the place she has learned to find and be her best self."

—SANDY YAKLIN, ACTON ACADEMY PARENT

A magical twist was happening in my personal Acton Academy story. With each month that passed, I was growing. And so were the other parents who had committed to this journey with me. As our children launched into their Hero's Journeys, we parents were becoming braver. We were learning to kill our tendencies to project our personal desires onto our children and to protect them from difficulty. We were becoming learners again. Even dreamers.

We parents at Acton Academy were stretching into our own inner selves to explore who *we* were meant to be. The children's curiosity began fueling our own. And our burgeoning curiosity was in turn fueling the children's wide-open dreaming about their futures. We had escaped the trap of stressing about homework, PTA politics, and grades on tests. Like freeing birds from cages, we were loosening our grip on our children and they were learning to fly. Once you experience such a thing, you really can't go back to a system that is built to keep unique individualities tamed, even dulled.

One morning at drop-off, I ran into Bodhi's mom, Becca, who said, "Seeing Bodhi become so self-motivated and independent is amazing. I only wish I could have trusted the process and not worried so much when he was in elementary school! Can you believe he just finished a 900-page book on the history of oil—that he chose to read—in THREE WEEKS?!?"

I was just beginning to see what was happening—parents who tasted Acton Academy wanted one for their own communities. We had seen this very early but never thought it would actually happen. Within one year of opening our doors, however, an old friend came knocking. Would we please let him start his own Acton Academy?

Acton Academy Guatemala City

When we were still in our second year, with Acton Academy up and running, Jeff received a phone message from Juan Bonifasi, one of his most successful students in the first graduating class of the Acton School of Business. Juan and his wife were visiting Austin from their native Guatemala City with their three children as part of a reunion weekend celebration with Juan's old Acton MBA friends. He'd heard we had started an elementary school and was deeply curious about Acton Academy. He shared his frustrations with the limited school opportunities for his own children back in Guatemala.

We invited him and Ana to meet us at Acton Academy, and they spent most of the day observing in the studio. At first they seemed overwhelmed as they watched children in constant motion without the direction of an adult. But Juan saw through what appeared to be chaos. Jeff had always described Juan as a "systems expert," and I was about to see that in action.

"Systems," he said. "I see layers of systems. I now understand why the children can function so freely together. It is because of the systems in place. The adults aren't managing the children. Systems are." He pointed to the schedule on the fridge, and then to the checklist for studio maintenance. He spent the most time looking at the big tracking sheet on the wall where the Eagles wrote their goals and posted their progress. Just like Heather and Allan Staker had noted after their tour, Juan saw everything in the rooms arranged in a way that not only felt good, but was logically organized and labeled so the children knew where everything they needed could be found. The Contract was posted. The rules of engagement for discussions were posted. There was a checklist for the first draft of short stories the children were working on. Just reading what was hanging on the walls could tell an observer exactly how the children functioned so independently in this space.

Ana and Juan looked like they were on a mission. They walked through our small schoolhouse and into the kitchen, where they saw plastic goggles hanging on hooks next to white lab coats, each with a nametag. Stacked on the floor were plastic bins with holes cut into them, white PVC pipes duct-taped into the holes, and buckets of water. There was a map on the wall marking the progress of the students' quest to discover the secrets of electricity. The display included the challenges for that afternoon: use water wheels to demonstrate voltage and amperage.

"Sounds like fun," Ana said as she took Juan's hand and led him to Charlie's desk.

"Charlie, would you show us what is in the blue sack hanging on everyone's chair?" she asked. Charlie, then eight years old and very serious about his work at Acton, pulled a blue binder from his sack and handed it to Mrs. Bonifasi.

"May we look through it?" she asked.

She and Juan read the first page. It was the worksheet the Eagles used to set and track their S.M.A.R.T. goals (for *specific, measurable, achievable, realistic, and time-bound*, as created by George T. Doran). I saw her point to the checkmarks where Charlie had charted his progress: *Done, In Progress, Not Started*. They thumbed through the rest of the binder's sections: reading, writing, math, projects. It was all there for an Eagle to manage.

"Thanks, Charlie," she said. "Looks like you have a lot going on."

They walked through the rooms, looking over the shoulders of Eagles as they worked on laptops or read books or jotted things down in their writers' notebooks. They then sat in a corner on pillows to watch the day roll on. I saw Juan jotting down notes in his own notebook. Ana stood up to read the student contract and rules of engagement framed and hanging on the wall.

Soon, Ellie held up a rain stick to signal the time for a change. It was the "anti-school-bell." The quiet sound of beads falling through the wooden cylinder was surprising in its gentleness and power. Rather than jolting students to attention, it coaxed them to focus on Ellie.

"Core skills time is over, and it's time to organize the studio," Ellie said in her quiet voice. "See you at the artichoke rug in fifteen minutes."

Juan and Ana watched the Eagles, ranging in age from six to ten years old, as they scrambled around, putting laptops into the charging cart, picking up trash on the floor, pushing chairs in under the table, and placing books back on the shelves. One Eagle took a clipboard off the wall in the library. Juan asked if he could see it. It was a checklist of what needed to be done at the end of core skills time.

"Ah," he said to me as I walked by, "the magic of checklists."

Within exactly fifteen minutes, the entire class was sitting in a circle on the artichoke rug, silently awaiting Anna's discussion question: "When did you find yourself in your panic zone today, and how did you get out of it and back into your challenge or comfort zone?"

For the next fifteen minutes, an engaged, rich discussion about work habits ensued.

The Bonifasis looked at each other, wide-eyed. All they said as I met them at the door was, "Wow."

. . .

A few hours later we sat in our living room with the Bonifasi family and watched the pink-and-orange sunset streaming through the windows.

"Tell us about Guatemala City," I said.

"Guatemala is a developing country," Juan explained, "but an increasingly vibrant one."

Juan said the heart of Guatemala City was like a free-market oasis. In fact, that is why he was able to cofound with Jeff and other entrepreneurs an Acton School of Business within the Francisco Marroquín University in Guatemala City. Juan valued the principles of freedom, truth, learning, and excellence. "It is the shared principles that bind us," he said. "I want for my children what I was able to experience as an adult under Jeff's teaching. Would you share this so we could open an Acton Academy?"

"So much of what we saw today in your classroom was different from anything we expected or had seen before," Ana added.

"And the children are so happy," Juan said.

We spent the next couple of hours trading our stories of school and learning. As they got up to leave, Jeff handed Juan a copy of Clark Aldrich's book *Unschooling Rules*.

"Juan and Ana, if anyone in the world could take what we have as a prototype and plant one elsewhere, it would be you," Jeff said. "We'd love to see you start your own Acton in Guatemala."

A month after their visit, Juan had already found families who would enroll their children. And with that, Acton Academy Guatemala City began to take shape.

· · ·

In January 2012, Jeff, Charlie, Sam, and I decided to venture to Guatemala to see how Juan and Ana were doing with their start-up Acton Academy. Because their oldest child was thirteen, they started both an elementary and middle school studio—they were ahead of us already. We couldn't wait to see what our school model looked like in a different culture and with a larger spread of ages.

From the airplane window, I could see the lush landscape hugging a volcano jutting up into the clouds just outside the city. This was my first visit to Guatemala, and bringing my children along as the expert ambassadors to our sister school was something I'd never imagined.

I had no idea what to expect. Jeff, who had visited Guatemala many times, had said only, "Get ready for the greatest hospitality you've ever experienced."

Hospitality aside, I wanted to see whether Acton Academy in Central America was a true reflection of our vision. Driving straight from the airport, we pulled up to a home surrounded by a wrought-iron fence. Inside the fence, lush landscaping with flowering vines draped the entry. Three Acton Eagles stood at the door with big smiles on their faces and their hands extended.

As we walked through the home-turned-school, things began to look familiar. There was a framed student contract on the wall. There was a Hero's Journey map. There was a chart of personal goals with marks showing progress. And when we walked onto the back porch, there stood thirty Eagles, ranging in age from four to thirteen years old. Everything was spoken and written in English. These children were bilingual—such an admirable discipline.

The rest of the day included a Skype session with our studio back home and observing their project time, a game-making quest. Charlie and Sam led the closing discussion of the day and asked the group which was more important—knowing you are on a Hero's Journey or being part of a tight-knit community. They facilitated the discussion like Socratic guides, going deeper into the answers, asking for examples, taking a vote, and then asking for final lessons learned.

I was seeing our model taking on a life of its own and children forming bonds based on shared principles and a culture that transcended national borders.

Acton Academy Venice Beach

Dani and Russ Foltz-Smith had moved to Austin in 2010 with their young girls, Bella and Reese. The California transplants knew nothing about local schools in our area. All they knew was that they were not going to send their children to a traditional public or private school. They had tried these and neither had worked for their daughters. Within a week of settling in Texas, they showed up on Acton Academy's doorstep.

Dani, tan from beach living and dressed a black sundress, described her frustration at trying to find a school that would keep her girls, then only six and eight, engaged in learning. She had read our website, watched Jeff's TEDx talk, and felt in her gut this was what she wanted her girls to experience. Russ, red-haired and quiet, gave me a bear hug as we finished our tour of Acton.

"What do we need to do to start tomorrow?" he asked.

Bella and Reese took to Acton Academy like eagles to the sky. But after only two years with us, California was calling them home. Russ's company decided to move him back to Venice Beach. Dani burst into my office with the news.

"Laura, I'm in a panic," she said. "I told him I don't want to go, because there is no Acton Academy there.

"Is there any way we could be commuter students? I can manage the online learning and then we could Skype in for Socratic discussions," she pleaded. It was the only way she could feel okay about leaving Austin.

"I'd love to try!" I said. "One idea is that their writing buddies could communicate their feedback by email. I think it could work if you keep up the goal-setting focus and accountability from your end."

"What about the projects?" Dani asked.

"You can create your own projects or you can use the ones we are doing," I replied. "We can send you the basic plan and you can adjust as needed."

Several good-bye parties later, we found ourselves with two Eagles attending our school from Venice Beach, California. We quickly discovered this was not a sustainable option. "They tried to live on Texas time in California," Dani told me after two weeks. "But it's just too tiring to get up that early for the morning group discussions. I have another crazy idea. Can I start my own Acton here?"

I was getting used to crazy ideas. Without much thought I said, "Sure, and you can call it Acton Academy Venice Beach!"

· · ·

Dani, Russ, and their girls had made it a tradition to visit our Acton campus during their spring break. This gave the girls the chance to work again with their original Acton friends, and Dani and I got to catch up on how her work was going. Acton Academy had taken on a life of its own under her leadership, but the shared core principles were driving it to success.

She had a small but thriving group of Eagles working from her home, doing core skills on their laptops in the mornings. They spent the afternoons tackling big-project work out in the community and often had PE on the beach. The library had become a favorite place for research and discovery and to fuel their writer's workshops.

"It's simple, but it feels like Acton. We've got that same joy of learning," Dani said.

Sharing tools for the journey

Were we going to actively spread the Acton Academy model or let it spread organically, like a grassroots movement? I remembered a Skype call I had that day with a young single woman in Denver, Samantha Simpson. She was applying to be our apprentice guide and closed the interview by saying, "It would be my dream to open my own Acton Academy someday." Open your own Acton? Something was happening that was bigger than the two of us. People were quietly waking up to a new idea of "school" and we just happened to be in a position to equip others to build their own. I shared this interview with Jeff and he said, "Should we plan for 100 more Acton Academies—or 1,000?"

Just when I was getting comfortable.

By our fourth year, there were four new Actons opening, and

we were receiving email requests every day for information on how to start a school. We were overloaded. I was laser-focused on problems in our elementary and middle school studios. Jeff was trying to figure out high school.

We needed help. This was like a grassroots movement and we were only barely able to support it. And the kit—our collection of projects, quests, processes, and systems for others to use—was, frankly, pitiful.

Our help came in the form of Matt Clayton, the cowriter of the Christensen Report who had set up the phone interview between Heather Staker and Jeff back in 2010. He also happened to be Heather's brother and had told her that since working on the report he could not get Acton Academy out of his mind.

At the time, he was engaged in a successful career at Goldman Sachs but was enthralled with the theory of disruption and, in particular, how it applied to education. We contacted Matt to see if we could lure him to come work with us in Austin. We got lucky.

In 2014, Matt moved to Austin with his new wife, Maria, to lead our expansion. As our lead evangelist, he would help us "bottle up" our processes, systems, methods, and learning design into a world-class kit to help others open their own Acton Academy.

Matt turned out to be the perfect fit for the job. Wicked smart, entrepreneurial, and bearing an impassioned dedication to change the concept of school forever, he took to Acton like, well, a hero to a journey.

Matt worked with software designers and interviewed Eagles on their work habits to help him build a software platform for

Acton students around the world to view their daily challenges, track their personal goals, post their work, receive critiques, and compile badges. Never in the world has anything so user-friendly and information-rich been given to young people and their parents to show—in real time—details about the learning process at school.

Matt also created a simple sales funnel for prospective new owners to follow in their quest to open a new school. Our criteria for accepting new owners once we knew they believed in the mission? Just two things: Their own children would attend their school, and they had experience running a successful small business or community project.

I overheard Matt on his phone in May 2017. It was a conversation I heard many times since he'd begun working with us. I knew it must have started on the other end of the phone with the questions "What is your kit?" and "Are you a franchise?"

Think of Acton Academy as a network of world-class entrepreneurs united around a mission of building schools for their children. Not a franchise, but a workshop. We share tools online via a program called Acton Toolshed, plus meeting for a yearly Acton Conference in Austin.

There are three main benefits to the Acton network:

1. *The people:* The people are the best part of Acton Academy. The online Owners Discussion Forum is rich in on-the-ground experience, with several threads each day. We've found that schools experience similar issues

across the network, so if you run into a problem or find something that really works, someone else is likely in the same boat. I could never oversell this group of people!

2. *The systems:* What Acton does better than anyone else in the world is build a studio where young people lead. These tools are all available to new Actons. So this includes tools for goal setting, Socratic discussions, studio maintenance, studio contracts, Eagle Bucks, our software platform, etc.

3. *Curriculum or Learning Design:* The biggest time-savers in the kit are all of the plug-and-play quests and projects developed over the years, the writing challenges, and civilization discussion material—all play-tested with Eagles in Austin.

In short, anyone looking to just "press play" like a franchise kind of school will likely be disappointed by what they find. But entrepreneurial parents who want a Hero's Journey with their children will find a deep well of high-quality tools.

Reassurance and belonging

Like the Children's Business Fair, which took on a life of its own and grew without our paying much attention to it, Acton Academy was lighting a fire in the bellies of parents who wanted something different from what conventional schools—public or private—were offering. They may never have imagined themselves as school administrators but were willing to take action on behalf of their children. After Guatemala City and Venice Beach, Acton Academies took root in Houston, Chicago, New Orleans, Toronto, Sacramento, Las Cruces (New Mexico), and forty other cities around the world.

Although we would not be graduating high school students until the spring of 2018, Acton Academy Guatemala City had already launched one of their Eagles into the world. Maria Theresa was simultaneously and successfully taking courses through Udacity, Coursera, and edX while serving as a consultant for her local university. She'd recently given a TEDx talk on the future of education.

"She is now the youngest person ever invited to Peter Thiel's 20 under 20 conference for the best and brightest youth in the world," Juan wrote. "And she believes that a Wikipedia-like revolution is coming, one where individual students will source, curate, and sequence videos, problems, simulations, projects, real-world challenges, and other learning experiences, with each student finding the pattern that works best for them for a particular knowledge area or skill."

Her analogy was DNA. Sequencing chunks of educational material is like sequencing genes: Each individual has a unique sequence that works best, but you can learn a great deal from sharing and studying the similarities and differences in the patterns and how they vary among different people. She designed a website where students share and compare different sequences for a variety of topics. In 2017, she took an apprenticeship with one of the top medical researchers in the world, looking for a cure for Lou Gehrig's disease.

"At the age of sixteen, Maria Theresa was accepted to the University of California at Berkeley," Juan said.

Our own Eagles began to feel part of something larger than our little campus. What Juan and Dani had started by taking Acton to their communities had rippled across the United States and beyond. And the Eagles felt the swell of opportunity. They were part of a global community.

CHAPTER 10

TREASURE FOUND

"Globally, every Acton Academy is different. While the systems are similar, almost everything else takes its own path because it reflects young heroes' choices and their journeys. Uniquely beautiful!"

—JIA-HONG TANG, OWNER OF ACTON ACADEMY KUALA LUMPUR, MALAYSIA

At 5:00 p.m. on March 5, 2017, I stood amid some 200 guests in our middle school studio. They had come to Austin from around the world for the annual South by Southwest (SXSW) festival—the largest music, film, education, and technology gathering on the planet. The SXSW crowd on our campus that evening was a mix of educators, innovators, artists, entrepreneurs, and foundation leaders, all curious about what it looked like inside Acton Academy, the small school turning heads as a disruptor in education. For the event, we had invited new Acton Academy owners from around the world to share their stories as a panel discussion after the social mingling.

I looked over at the world map hanging on the studio wall. There were forty-seven bright-pink sticky notes marking new Acton Academy locations around the United States and in

Canada, Guatemala, El Salvador, Malaysia, Honduras, Panama, England, and beyond.

Thinking back to 2009, when I sat with seven children and two guides on our green artichoke rug, I laughed to myself. The scene before me had never been in our plans. We were simply doing what we thought was best for our own children, building the airplane as we flew it, each day writing a plan for the next, and hoping our seven Acton Eagles would remain airborne.

Acton Academy had grown beyond our sweet schoolhouse into something far greater. And this growth had nothing to do with us. The Acton story was not our story anymore. It wasn't even a story about school, really. This story was about the unstoppable human spirit and the belief parents—from all walks of life and in all cultures—hold dear. They believe their children deserve to find a calling and experience life as a Hero's Journey, an adventure filled with love, passion, meaning, and joy.

Although each Acton Academy has its own look and feel, there is something unmistakably shared—and you can feel it when you walk into any one of them. It's a spark of positive energy that the children exhibit, no matter what time of day it is. "Why are the children so happy here?" one of the guests asked me.

I quoted Matt Clayton's first comment when he saw the children on our campus. "Because freedom is ennobling."

. . .

A panel of brave souls

The guests saw Jeff step up to the row of seven stools placed in the front of the studio. They quickly became quiet as he cleared his throat.

"You are standing on sacred ground," he said. "This is where learning is treasured and honored above all else. The Acton Eagles have claimed it as their own and protect it fiercely. We are all guests here, including Laura and me.

"I've invited a few brave souls to come forward and sit on these stools. They have started their own learner-driven communities—their own Acton Academies—with only a kit that's still in development, a set of promises, some shared principles, and—most important—a shared belief that every child is a genius. Please welcome some of our Acton Academy owners from around the world."

Jeff introduced them, stepped aside, and said, "They're all yours. This is your chance to ask them anything."

The questions started flying.

"Why did you open an Acton Academy?"

Joey Bynum, co-owner with his wife, Jayme, of Acton Academy West Austin, jumped at the opportunity to share his story. "I was getting my MBA at the Acton School of Business back in 2013. We were sharing the campus with the Acton Academy," he said. "At the time, Jayme and I were looking for a place for our son to go to school," he continued, "and I was thinking, wow, these young kids at Acton Academy are doing things that I'm just learning, and I'm getting my MBA! Why aren't kids doing this kind of learning earlier?"

That question was enough for Joey and Jayme to launch Austin's second Acton Academy.

Our old friends, Juan and Ana Bonifasi, sat on stools next to Joey and described why they had taken Acton to Guatemala. Next to Juan sat Mike Olson from Talent Unbound, the Acton affiliate in Houston. Tall and lean, Mike spoke quickly and could barely contain his optimism.

"When I looked at the opportunities my kids had in the traditional system, they would have done just fine. They would have gotten decent grades, played sports, and gone to college. But I looked at the future and the economy that is coming and our assumptions about the future—how those are going to change with artificial intelligence and automation."

He said he saw the gap widening at a very fast pace between the traditional skills children are taught in a traditional system and what they will need.

"I wanted my children to be in a place where there is creativity, independence, and freedom," he said. "I wanted open-endedness. I wanted them dealing with frustration, ambiguity. I wanted them to chart their own path."

Rob Huge, dressed in a long-sleeved plaid shirt and khaki slacks, jumped in: "Don't tell my kids this, but I didn't do it for them."

The audience laughed.

Rob named his Acton affiliate in Chicago "Greenfields Academy." It was thriving with a pre-K, elementary, and middle school. "I wanted to spend my time working on something that was going to have a significant impact on the world."

An arm shot up from the back of the studio. "What misconceptions about Acton Academy do you face?"

Veronica Klugman, an Acton owner from Tegucigalpa, Honduras—her shiny, straight black hair falling below her shoulders—sat still and erect on her stool. Though soft-spoken and unassuming, she commands respect with her rational, direct style.

"People say we don't give grades," she said. "But we do. Every grade we give is A+, because until a child masters something, they do not move on. It's not enough to get 80 percent on a math test. That's not mastery. A hundred percent proves you have mastered the skill."

Joey added, "I've dealt with the misconception that people think life at Acton is one of the extremes—either that the kids are swinging from the branches, just playing around, or the extreme of overly rigorous academics that are micromanaged. Neither is true."

Mark Klugman, Veronica's husband and co-owner of Acton Academy Honduras, sat among the guests, his wooden walking stick next to his chair, and jumped in, further describing the feel of an Acton Academy.

"Acton is in motion," he said. "If you look at a Montessori school or a traditional school, not much has changed in the last fifty years. But at Acton, we are changing as fast as your cellphone changes, because that's how the world works. There is no bureaucracy. This is a conscious directive for the model so we can always be changing. The only thing that remains the same across the board is the principles."

The next question came: "What type of parents do you attract?"

"About one-third of our parents come from public schools, one-third from private, and one-third from homeschool backgrounds," answered Mike.

Juan's response was less quantitative. "Responsible parents—parents who want to take responsibility for their own learning and their children's learning," he said.

Jeff added to this: "We ask children *and* parents to be on their own Hero's Journeys. The ones who don't want that leave—because it's really hard work to choose the path of a hero. The Hero's Journey is simple. It means when you fail, you get back up and get in the game again. Heroes don't always win, but they do get back up. Parents who are ready to allow their children to fail, have a hard time, and then give them a hug, saying, 'I love you, now back in you go'—these are the parents for us."

A tall man with a shaved head and graying beard, his SXSW name badge affixed to his black leather jacket, asked, "What is the mind shift for the kids who come here for the first time from a traditional school?"

"We call it 'freedom shock,'" Rob responded. "They just come in and wait around for someone to tell them what to do. When a kid walks into this from a traditional setting where they are told exactly what to do and when, we've calculated it takes about a month for every year they have spent in that environment to start thriving in ours."

Joey's story brought back memories from our first years of middle school. "They start out skeptical," he said. "They look around and see there is an adult, an authority, in the room. And they think at some point that person is going to step in and tell them to either do or not do something. Then they are surprised when their neighbor, another student, says, 'Hey, you are violating the contract that's hanging on the wall. You owe me an Eagle Buck for that.' After that, they never look at the adult in the room again."

Ana Bonifasi spoke next: "Our daughter, Isabella, two months into Acton Academy after coming from traditional schooling, thanked us. She said, 'Mom and Dad, thank you for starting Acton. For the first time, I'm thinking for myself.'" This drew applause from the crowd.

After several more questions, Jeff looked at the clock. It was time to wrap things up. We had time for one more question.

"How does this work with children who have learning challenges?"

Jeff estimated that perhaps one-third of our Eagles have some level of ADD or ADHD. They often just need to move around or change tasks in order to work hard.

"We also have children with mild dyslexia. We aren't experts, and when professional intervention is necessary, we work with the parents to figure out how the child can remain in the studio and gain the after-school or at-home support to continue progressing and participating within the studio contract."

Veronica shared her story: "I think many learning challenges are related to stress the children feel," she said. "We had a student who every ten minutes did a cartwheel. We wondered whether her other school, which was very traditional, allowed this. They did not. So what did she do instead? She said, 'I bit my tongue.'

"After three months with us at Acton, she doesn't do cartwheels anymore, and she certainly doesn't have to bite her tongue to keep from moving," Veronica said. "She came to us in the second grade and didn't know how to add, because all of her energy was spent trying to deal with her stress. Now, she's a whiz at math and is learning."

"How do you convince parents who believe in traditional school to come here?"

The owners all looked at each other. Almost in unison they said, "We don't."

I realized what Jeff and I had done in starting Acton Academy. All we really did was deliver a simple message: *There is a new idea. It works.*

Others are now taking the torch and carrying it to light up nooks and crannies in far-off places.

An unlikely treasure found (and a little magic for parents)

The social gathering of our curious SXSW guests spurred my pondering. While I'm fascinated and energized by the questions that continue to arise during this journey—questions about human motivation, culture, and learning itself—there is a treasure I've discovered that affects the rest of my life.

It is not a treasure I sought. Nor is it one I wanted. It does not include riches or comforts or successes or anything to do with the ecstasy of life and learning. My treasure is all about the agony. I have finally discovered on a personal level what *passion* truly means and I want nothing less than to embrace it. It means there will be suffering along the road. I don't *want* suffering. But it is a necessary part of the true experience of passion. I will no longer work to avoid it and I will no longer fear it.

This treasure has become my magic mantra not only for building a learning community but also for being a happy, thriving parent. I can now say with conviction, "Struggle will teach you the best things about yourself."

If children are given room to struggle and to figure things out on their own, and if they have support from a mentor, peer, or guide who knows them well and holds them accountable, they will learn more than we can imagine.

How can I make this kind of room? I must remember to step back. Wait to be surprised instead of right. Only then will I discover the wonderment of daily life.

This is abundance. It is the essence of a Hero's Journey—and a biological and spiritual truth of being human.

I was able to learn this for only one reason. And it was our very first idea. The most upside-down, audacious idea of them all: Trust the children.

HOMECOMING

The SXSW event was over. The sun had set on our campus and the studio was empty and quiet. But the air had a fullness to it. The energy of thinking, creative people mixed up together to celebrate the wonder of learning lingered on.

I turned off the studio lights and walked to my car alone. Like all good introverts, I craved the silence of the drive home after the intense interaction of the day. I expected this moment would be a happy one. A peaceful one. We'd accomplished a lot.

But it wasn't. I felt a homesickness that I couldn't pin down. What was this "missing" feeling?

It was Charlie.

Now more than ever, I missed him at Acton.

Listening to all of the other Acton stories and witnessing so many people embracing innovation in education made his move away from it hurt even more. How could *he* not be experiencing this? Why is *he* sitting at a desk being lectured to all day?

In the months Charlie had been gone, he'd lost his love of reading, a tragedy I could barely stand. And he'd become worried about points on quizzes—like knowing the year Shakespeare was born. He'd also become highly stressed over missing any school—even if it was to go paragliding, his one true passion. He'd gotten his solo license as a thirteen-year-old, and zipping off for a four-day weekend was a natural opportunity when he attended Acton, just like other Eagles would take off if they got the lead part in a local play or had the opportunity to travel with family. "Five points off my total average," he told me, "if I miss one more day of school."

Sadder for me was learning that he feared taking a divergent stand in discussions at his new school. "The teacher has a right and wrong answer for discussions. If you take a stand for the side he sees as 'wrong,' he corrects you," he explained. He went on to describe how students immediately ask the teacher the meaning of a reading selection if they did not understand it. And the teacher would give the answer. There was no struggling to try to figure it out and debate ideas among themselves.

At Acton, learning to disagree respectfully—and be disagreed with—is one of the great assurances of the Socratic discussions.

On the other hand, I saw how well he adjusted to teachers and assignments in the larger school. He'd proven to himself that he was fully capable of learning in a traditional atmosphere. He could walk into a room of people he didn't know and survive just fine. He could make friends and compete on the soccer field and the track. He was making straight As.

"It's his feeling of inadequacy that breaks my heart," Jeff said. "Never has my son felt inadequate until he was in the system based on memorization, obedience, and standardized sorting of intellect."

I reminded myself that this was Charlie's journey. And as I've said to so many parents over the years, "Each person has their own journey. Acton Academy is not always it."

. . .

I pulled into my driveway. The lights were on in the kitchen, and I saw Sam and Charlie sitting and talking at the kitchen table, where we'd planned the first Children's Business Fair, which has now, like Acton, taken on a life of its own. We had more than 1,000 shoppers at 115 booths in our front yard this year. We built a kit for that, too, and now there are more than fifty Children's Business Fairs around the country.

I turned off the engine and sat in the dark, looking at them through the window. *This has been a messy adventure,* I thought. In the early Acton years, I was playing either offense or defense, pushing forward or fighting off naysayers and doubters. I wish I had known to love the messiness, ambiguity, and questions. Instead, I felt miserable as I overexplained our idea and methods to parents, neighbors, and friends.

It took the children—the Acton Eagles—rising to the occasion, embracing freedom and responsibility with gusto, to set me free. It was the children who taught me how to be a parent. They were the ones who had the courage to grow.

. . .

Three days later, Jeff and Charlie took off for a four-day paragliding trip during Charlie's spring break. Sunday night, when they arrived back home, I saw that old look in Charlie's eyes again, that look of exhilaration and clarity that he seemed to have more often in the early Acton days. He had again tasted the thrill of flight and couldn't wipe the smile off his face as he described his long weekend. Now *that's* the Charlie I had been missing—free and living large, unafraid, and willing to leap off mountains to get what he wanted.

But reality hits hard. We went to bed, and in a blink the alarm was going off at 5:45 a.m. There was no denying the fact that spring break was over. It was time to get Charlie back to his tightly managed school life.

We drove to school in silence, and I dropped him off with a heavy heart. His lips formed a tight, straight line—a look of resignation.

"I love you, Charlie."

"Thanks, Mom," he said. "See you later."

I picked him up at 3:15, following the routine I had grown to accept and love, because it meant thirty-minute car rides with just me and Charlie—treasured time alone with my son. We listened to talk radio, the hosts hashing out the Austin City Council's ongoing battle to try to bring affordability and calmer traffic to a city that continues to boom. *Charlie's love of political banter hasn't waned,* I thought to myself as he engaged aloud in an argument with the voices on the radio.

When we pulled into the driveway, Jeff's car was already there.

"He's home early," I said to Charlie.

"Good," he replied.

He hopped out of the car and beat me inside as I picked up the mail and patted the dogs. By the time I entered the kitchen, our world had taken a turn I had not allowed myself to imagine.

"He's leaving that school," Jeff said.

"What?" I asked, dumbfounded.

"It's true, Laura, he just told me," Jeff said. "Charlie's coming back to the Acton way."

Charlie had simply walked in the door and told Jeff that he wanted to go to back to real apprenticeships, online learning, reading more deep books and writing something worth publishing. He told him he wanted to get his pilot's license when he turned sixteen and go to college after high school. He said he thought he could do more than just sit in class to get there.

With that, I dropped the mail and my bag on the floor. I walked straight to Jeff. We held each other, shaking our heads in wonder. Charlie had done what he set out to do. He needed to know he could learn from teachers, take tests, and meet college preparatory standards. He had tested himself and now he was coming home. The school his parents founded finally made sense in real terms to this young man.

Taite, too, had needed to break away to discover more about herself. She was heading to college and joining us for weekly family dinners, reconnecting with her brothers and opening up to us about her dreams and fears.

Through it all, Sam had continued being our steady force in the studios and at home. Not everyone must leave to discover who they are.

And Charlie chose to wait and tell his father first. He could have told me on the way home that afternoon or waited until I walked in the door, but he wanted Jeff to hear it from him first, and alone. The meaning of that was not lost on me. What a gift to a father who had mourned what felt like the loss of his son for months. This was a gift well given upon the return of a hero from his journey.

Now Charlie could take the reins of his education back, drive his learning, and follow his dreams. Now he was free.

Better yet, now he could fly.

ACKNOWLEDGMENTS

I am merely the vessel that lets the Acton story pour forth into the world. This book would not have happened without the following people who have taught me so much.

Harry Jaffe pulled the story out of me with his relentless questions and kind patience. I thank him for encouraging my writing and fighting for my story. I am indebted to Clint Greenleaf, a generous genius who works harder than most humans and made this book a physical reality.

Ken DeCell, Jane Rosenman, Sheila Parr, Thom Lemmons, Elizabeth Brown, Sheila Youngblood, and Reese Youngblood taught me that life is much better with editors and designers. If you get to work with more than one, you are beyond lucky. These hard-working, generous, and talented people lifted my writing and book design to a better place.

Marcy Carpenter, Jeff Carpenter, Becca Cody, Divit Tripathi, Lauren Kubacki, Yolanda King, and Kelvin King are long-time Acton Academy parents who met with me to share their personal stories. They are examples of people who are unafraid to learn, love, and grow right alongside their children. I thank them for being my fellow travelers on this journey. I'll not forget what Kelvin said when he reflected on his first time at an Acton Academy open house: "I looked around the room for a face that looked like my own. I didn't see one. But then I looked more and saw world maps, globes, and statements of Acton's principles. We came to this school not because we look alike or live the same way but because we believe in the same fundamental principles of freedom, justice, and individual worth. We are bound by what we believe, not by our heritage." I believe this is the reason our idea is spreading beyond our own community and country.

My dear sisters and beloved friends—Kirstin Lee, Michelle Webb, Nicole Barr, Laurie Haddow, and Caroline Wilson—held up the light that brought me home when I got stuck in the dark woods. I thank them for not letting me stay there and hide.

Acton Academy reflects more of my parents, Mike and Joanna Anderson, than they will ever know. Their trust and belief in me was the starting point for this work. Even though my mother didn't live long enough to see it come to fruition, her spirit of joyful adventure runs throughout this story. I gave my father the painful task of reading the first draft of my manuscript. Poor man. I thank him for the gentle and honest feedback that directed me to start over.

I thank Lolly Anderson for helping me pin down a decision on the design of the book's cover and for her reliable ability to help me unwind and laugh. I thank her for encouraging me at every turn.

Heather and Allan Staker are rock stars in my world. Words can't adequately express my gratitude for their willingness to uproot their large family and join this journey without knowing where it would lead. I thank them for sharing their personal story with generosity and for taking the Children's Business Fair kit into the world.

Matt and Maria Clayton persisted in encouraging me to write this story down. I thank them for their never-ending belief in the Acton ideals and their insistence that others need to hear the story of our origin. The world is better because these two are in it. I am beholden to their unwavering optimism.

I thank Bodhi, Ellie, Chris, Cash, Saskia, and Libby for allowing me to shine a little more light on their own journeys. These young people will change the world.

If there was wind beneath my wings to get this job done, it came from the brilliant minds and vast spirits of heroes whose thinking I savor reading and listening to: Steven Tomlinson, Clark Aldrich, Sugata Mitra, Seth Godin, Tom Vander Ark, Bernard Bull, Ted Dintersmith, Dan Peters, Kimberly Watson-Hemphill, Clayton M. Christensen, Jane McGonigal, Salman Khan, Carol Dweck, and Maria Montessori, to name a few.

Juan and Ana Bonifasi and Dani and Russ Foltz-Smith were the brave people who allowed me to walk with them and share their stories of being pioneers using our start-up kit in its very early days—which really wasn't a kit at all but a stack of unorganized papers. I will always be grateful to and surprised by them.

I thank the new Acton Academy owners around the world, now too many to mention in this small space. Every single day they look into the eyes of children and say, "You are very special. You have gifts within you that the world needs." And then they set them free to find those gifts. They took our idea and made it so much better. The world needs this group's courage and perseverance.

Our current Austin team, so deeply committed to our mission, reveals to me each day that when adults step back, children rise up as heroes. They gave me time and space away from campus to get this book finished and cheered me on at every turn. I thank Samantha Jansky, Janita Lavani, Reed Youngblood, Rob Bakhshai, Justin Moss, Chase Pattillo, and Ben Bazan.

Rachel Davison Humphries, Kaylie Dienelt Reed, and Anna Blabey Smith were our team members in the very early days of Acton Academy. They said yes to the journey without any idea what they were getting into and were integral to our development. How could I have been so lucky to work among such wonderful people?

And nothing good happens in the world without the artists. Since our first year, two in particular have helped us pave a new way to grow the creative minds and spirits of children. Nat Miller sparks curiosity and joy through the theatrical arts. Zoey Upshaw's love and creative vision calls up the inner artist in each Eagle. I am grateful they were brave enough to experiment alongside us.

Underlying this book is a cloud of courageous souls—the parents and children who have joined Acton Academy over the years. Whether they are still with us or not, we have learned so much from each one. I thank them for believing in an idea that rides on the themes of love, trust, risk, reward, freedom, and responsibility.

Our children—Charlie, Sam, and Taite—are the reason Acton Academy exists. I thank them for being my sounding boards, my laughter, and my teachers. I thank them for listening to the discerning voices in their hearts and using them to challenge and change me. I thank them for being humble enough to be vulnerable and give me permission to share their personal stories. I couldn't be more grateful for who they are and that I get to live life with them. I love each of them beyond measure.

The way Jeff Sandefer loves me gives me courage to grow. I thank him for pushing me and pulling me through the process of getting our story on paper. It's a miracle we found each other on this Earth and I thank God each day for such a crazy gift.

Since the dawn of time and until the end of days, there will be some humans who simply can't stand the haunting of a calling and so end up saying, "Yes." As a citizen of the world, I am grateful.

ACTON ACADEMY'S MISSION, PROMISES, *and* BELIEFS

OUR MISSION:

We believe each person who enters Acton Academy will find a calling that changes the world.

OUR PROMISES:

We promise through Socratic guiding and experiential learning to encourage each member of our community to:

Begin a Hero's Journey

Discover one's own precious gifts and a commitment to mastery

Become a curious, independent, lifelong learner

Embrace the forging of a strong character

Cherish the arts, the physical world, and the mysteries of life

Treasure economic, political, and religious freedom

OUR BELIEFS:

> We believe each person has a gift that can change the world in a profound way.
>
> We believe in learning to learn, learning to do, and learning to be.
>
> We believe in a closely connected family of lifelong learners.
>
> We believe in economic, political, and religious freedom.

OUR EDUCATIONAL PHILOSOPHY:

We believe clear thinking leads to good decisions, good decisions lead to the right habits, the right habits forge character, and character determines destiny.

OUR ECONOMIC MODEL:

We believe self-directed, peer-to-peer learner-driven communities built by our young heroes will deliver transformational learning at a cost almost all parents can afford. At our campus in Austin, Texas, we set our tuition just under market value for private schools. For an eleven-month school year, our families pay just under $10,000. We are a 501(c)(3) organization; however, each Acton Academy is free to set up their business model and tax status independently.

OUR STUDIO-SIZE MODEL:

We believe Maria Montessori's model for an ideal classroom size with mixed ages works. She said, "We consider that in its best condition, the class should have between 28 and 35 children, but there may be even more in number." With that in mind, we designed each Acton Academy studio (elementary school, middle school, and high school) to host thirty-six students with a master guide and apprentice guide, understanding that the most important teaching will happen between peers in small, mixed-age groups.

ACTON ACADEMY STUDENT CONTRACT
2009–2010

I am on a Hero's Journey.

Even through hard times, I will not give up, because I have courage.

I will be honest with myself and others about the way I lead this journey.

I will try my hardest to reach all of my goals and I will make new goals as well.

I will try new things I have never done before, even things I might not be good at, to discover new talents.

I will encourage other people on their journeys but make sure they want and need my help.

I will take care of the things around me that help me learn and live.

I will take care of my body, my brain, and my heart by giving them the things they need to be healthy and grow, such as exercise, information, challenges, and love.

I will never give up on myself.

THE HERO'S JOURNEY

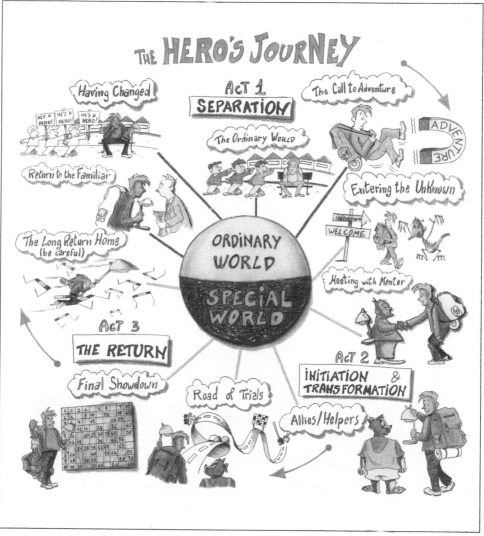

Illustration by Bruno lubrano Di Giunno

ACTON ACADEMY
Reading List for Parents

- **Unschooling Rules**, Clark Aldrich
- **NurtureShock**, Po Bronson
- **An Ethic of Excellence**, Ron Berger
- **The 3 Big Questions for a Frantic Family**, Patrick Lencioni
- **The Gifts of Imperfection**, Brené Brown
- **The One World Schoolhouse**, Salman Khan
- **Mindset**, Carol S. Dweck
- **Your Three-Year-Old**, Louise Bates Ames, PhD (*Each book for each age*)
- **A Thomas Jefferson Education**, Oliver DeMille
- **The Talent Code**, Daniel Coyle
- **Choice Words**, Peter H. Johnston
- **The Price of Privilege**, Madeline Levine, PhD
- **Montessori: The Science Behind the Genius**, Angeline Stoll Lillard

- **10 Conversations You Need to Have with Your Children**, Shmuley Boteach
- **The Smartest Kids in the World and How They Got That Way**, Amanda Ripley
- **Getting Smart**, Tom Vander Ark
- **Mastery: The Keys to Success and Long-Term Fulfillment**, George Leonard
- **2,002 Ways to Show Your Kids You Love Them**, Cyndi Haynes
- **Influencer**, Kerry Patterson, et al.
- **Crucial Conversations**, Kerry Patterson, et al.
- **The Dream Manager**, Matthew Kelly
- **Most Likely to Succeed**, Tony Wagner, Ted Dintersmith
- **The Gift of Fear**, Gavin de Becker
- **The Happiness Hypothesis**, Jonathan Haidt
- **Reality Is Broken**, Jane McGonigal
- **Blended: Using Disruptive Innovation to Improve Schools,** Michael Horn, Heather Staker, and Clayton M. Christensen
- **Ungifted: Intelligence Redefined**, Scott Barry Kaufman
- **Stop Stealing Dreams,** Seth Godin

THOUGHTS *on* GUIDING MATH SOCRATICALLY
by Jeff Sandefer

INTRODUCTION

The goal of Socratic guiding is to help someone else learn to think more clearly. In other words, questions and struggles are more important than answers.

KEYS TO THE SOCRATIC METHOD

Following are some of the keys to the Socratic method in math:

No shortcuts. Someone has to do the basic work first. Ask, "Have you watched the videos on Khan Academy?" and, "What example problems have you tried?" before you sit down to guide. If the person hasn't done the work, you cannot help them.

Remember that the goal of a Socratic question is *not* to help someone get the right answer. It's to help walk alongside someone, while they learn to think more clearly and critically.

Good Socratic questions focus on the process of solving a problem or making choices, never on answers.

EXAMPLE OF SOCRATIC QUESTIONS

- Is the problem being solved simple or complex?

- Can you restate the problem in your own words? What information do you know? What information are you trying to find out? Why does it matter?

- Is it harder to set up the problem correctly or solve it once it is set up?

- Are there few or many steps required to solve the problem?

- What's the hardest step in setting up the problem?

- Do you need to keep track of intermediate answers in an organized way? How will you do this?

- Is your biggest challenge not understanding the process, or is it carefully keeping track of the arithmetic so you don't make any careless mistakes?

- Do you find this skill particularly hard or easy? Why?

- What other math skill does this resemble? Why?

- How might you use this in the real world?

- What are the next steps you will take to master this problem?

- Is there a distraction I can help you remove so you can solve this?

- Are you in the right frame of mind to tackle this problem? If not, what needs to change? Should you set a deadline and a time to study for yourself?

SOCRATIC DISCUSSION RULES OF ENGAGEMENT

- Be on time and prepared.
- Listen intently.
- Take a stand.
- Build on previous comments.
- Be concise.
- Provide evidence or examples.

CONVERSATION *with* STEVEN TOMLINSON, *PhD,* MASTER SOCRATIC TEACHER

Q: Why teach with only questions, never answers?

ST: A good question inspires learning.

Q: But what is inspiration?

ST: It's the fusion of direction and motivation—and the energy released.

Q: Where does direction come from?

ST: Signs carefully placed by someone who has already explored the path.

Q: And motivation?

ST: From the joy of discovery and the desire to know and from the will to be both playful and powerful, like the teacher who asks questions before knowing the answers.

Q: What is a good question?

ST: Take some missing piece of the puzzle and hold it up to
the light. "What about *this*?"
Follow them off the path, into the thicket. "Where are
we headed? How far can we go?"
Call for courage. "Which one will you choose?"

Q: How do I become a good teacher?

ST: What sort of answer are you looking for? Before tech-
nique comes *intention*. Give up on impressing students.
Give up on helping them.
Commit to *be with* them and enjoy them and risk
learning alongside them.

OVERVIEW *of the* ACTON ACADEMY MIDDLE SCHOOL
and Launchpad Badge System

Introduction

The goal of Acton Academy Middle School and Launchpad (High School) is to retain the option for qualified Eagles to attend a selective college while preparing them for their next adventure in life. As part of this, Eagles must earn badges that can be reassembled into a traditional transcript required for college admission. They must also answer four important questions:

WHO AM I?

What are my gifts, skills, passions, next steps? What drives me? How do I best learn? How will I nurture and protect my inner life and health?

WHERE IS MY PLACE?

Do I have a deep understanding of the world? Given the lessons of history, economics, politics, and geography, where will I live, and how do I fit in and stand out?

WHAT IS MY "CALLING"?

What will be my next adventure in life, and how will I use my gifts and passion to solve a deep, burning need in the world?

WHO WILL I SERVE AS A LEADER?

Do I have the questions, tools, and skills I need to become a "level five" leader, form healthy relationships, and negotiate and solve disputes?

The badge system supports the journey of self-discovery, mastery, searching for a calling, and leadership in three main ways:

Self-Directed Learning: Because of the modular design and freedom for Eagles to make choices in the badge system, Eagles are able to customize their learning and move through subjects at their own pace. This freedom and the frequent celebrations when Eagles earn badges keep motivation and curiosity high. The requirement to self-manage time and set long-term goals, while difficult at times, may be the most important outcome of a badge system.

Accountability and Quality: Badges make it easier for Eagles and parents to track individual learning and monitor quality.

Ability to Prove Mastery to Others: Badges may be used in a portfolio to land a transformational apprenticeship or impress a college recruiter. In addition, the achievements within a badge can be rearranged into a traditional high school transcript to satisfy college admissions, without these traditional requirements diminishing the learning that occurs at Acton.

A Description of the Individual Badges

As part of celebrating the learning that occurs at Acton Academy, work is collected in the following badges, which can then be presented in the form of a traditional high school transcript or displayed in an electronic portfolio. (Eagles have detailed descriptions of each badge in the Electronic Points Tracker.)

CORE SKILLS

Math Badges from Khan Academy in pre-algebra, algebra I and II, geometry, trigonometry, pre-calculus, and calculus are the backbone for Acton Academy mathematics.

Deep Book Badges show an Eagle has devoured a "world-changing" or "life-changing" book and delivered a pitch designed to convince others to read it.

Genre and Three-Draft Genre Badges celebrate a significant achievement in writing, video, or another form of communication; a Three-Draft Genre (Revision) Badge includes at least three drafts plus associated critiques.

Civilization Badges equip Eagles with the tools, hard questions, and lessons that come from studying the lives of heroes, history, geography, economics, and philosophy, while exposing them to the collective memory of the human race.

QUESTS, QUEST CREATION, AND APPRENTICESHIPS

Quests and Quest Creation Badges: A Quest is a five- to seven-week series of challenges connected by a narrative and leading to a public exhibition of completed work; these are designed to deliver twenty-first-century skills in science and other real-world subjects. Quest Creation is the process of deep learning that a Launchpad Eagle undertakes not only to master a subject but also to create a Quest for other students to take.

Apprenticeship Badges celebrate real-world apprenticeships that help Eagles discover their next "stepping-stone adventure" and prepare them for a calling in life.

LEARNING BADGES

Learning Badges signify earning certain leadership privileges, from becoming an Independent Learner all the way through a Level Five Leader.

Ensuring Quality

Eagles set and often revisit the quality of standards for work submitted for badges. In most cases, a badge must be approved by a Running Partner or committee, using one or more of the following standards of excellence:

Best Work—If this is the first time someone has attempted a task, that person must certify it was their best work.

Better Than Last Time—If this is a task or skill that has been tried before, is there evidence of improvement?

Comparison to World-Class Standards—Is there a detailed critique comparing the work favorably to a world-class example?

Winner of a Contest—Did Eagles select this as a "best of" example in a vote by the studio?

Approved for Exhibition—Was this approved for exhibition to the public?

From time to time, an audit committee will be asked to check the ratings offered by Running Partners or committees. If there is evidence of a serious slide in quality or intentional misrepresentation, both the Eagle involved and those who previously approved the work will lose an entire badge, and an honor code violation may be taken to Council.

All systems can be cheated. Cheating is rampant in traditional schools and in the very best universities. Eagles will no doubt make mistakes, but in our system leaders understand that any decrease in quality in the badge system will throw their own work in doubt, so we expect to have a self-enforcing ethic in the community, as long as parents will respect the result.

LIST *of* ONLINE LEARNING PROGRAMS

Acton Academy has used the following online programs:

MATH

Khan Academy

DreamBox

ST Math

ALEKS

Mangahigh

READING

ClickN READ

Lexia

ReadTheory

Newsela

GRAMMAR/SPELLING/WRITING

Typing Club

VocabularySpellingCity

ClickN SPELL

NoRedInk

Grammarly

Storybird

PaperRater

FOREIGN LANGUAGE

Rosetta Stone

Mango Languages

Duolingo

OTHER

ChessKid

Codecademy

Algodoo and CK-12

GitHub and Code.org

Robo Rush

Cha-Ching

3D GameLab

Gamestar Mechanic

Tinkercad

VIA COURSERA

"Internet History, Technology, and Security"—University of Michigan

"An Introduction to American Law"—University of Pennsylvania

"Introduction to Chemistry: Reactions and Ratios"—Duke University

ABOUT *the* AUTHOR

Laura Anderson Sandefer lives in Austin, Texas, with her children, husband, and three dogs. She calls herself the Chief Encourager of the Acton Academy affiliation of independent schools. She'd love to hear from you if you are interested in starting your own Acton Children's Business Fair or an Acton Academy in your community. Feel free to email her at lsandefer@actonmail.org.